LARRY HAGMAN
A Biography

LARRY HAGMAN
A Biography

Leon Adams

St. Martin's Press
New York

Library of Congress Cataloging in Publication Data

Adams, Leon.
  Larry Hagman.

  1. Hagman, Larry.   2. Moving-picture actors and actresses—United States—Biography.   I. Title.
  PN2287.H17A63   1987   791.45′028′0924   [B]   86-26266
  ISBN 0-312-00137-1

First Edition

10 9 8 7 6 5 4 3 2 1

For Oma

CONTENTS

ACKNOWLEDGMENTS

The author wishes to acknowledge the gracious assistance of *Houston Chronicle* television critic Anne Hodges and *Austin American-Statesman* television critic Diane Holloway. Thanks are especially due photo researcher Amanda Rubin for her efforts in accumulating the pictures for this biography.

J.R. Ewing: A Global Mythology

You know, I'm often asked what are the sociological implications
of a guy like me becoming a national sex symbol, and I'll tell you
exactly what it means: the world is falling apart!

—Larry Hagman

Southern expressions are seldom used as often as the outside world might imagine. Nonetheless, from time to time
a Southerner can actually be heard to describe the
boundlessness of a full moon, a rich man's house, or a
lover's heart in the following manner: "Big. Big as
Dallas."

With apologies to all things enormous, let it be established from the outset: J.R. Ewing of the television series
"Dallas" is *bigger* than Dallas. The man so many love to
hate is bigger than Dallas, bigger than America and,
viewed from a certain angle, bigger than the world as we
know it today.

The matter is not one of television ratings, but rather
of mythology. These days, television has made it possible

for anyone—mayors, gymnasts, guitarists, car dealers—to appear "larger than life." It's one thing to capture the public's imagination, and quite another to enter the vocabulary of living things.

"Dallas" is shown in ninety-one countries, and in the words of one journalist, "has rearranged the daily lives of millions of people." To what extent? Consider:

—In the United Kingdom, some 20 million BBC-TV viewers watch "Dallas" . . . a number, incidentally, that exceeds the number of television sets in England. BBC paid $29,000 per episode in 1983 and $44,000 in 1985, but that still didn't seem enough to the U.S. distributors. Aware of the show's grip on the British, they instigated an unprecedented (for genteel England) bidding war between BBC and an independent station in the fall of 1985, touching off months of chaotic fisticuffs usually associated with mutinies. In the meantime, the deprived British public clamored loudly for the return of their beloved "Dallas." BBC finally gave in and matched the other station's higher offer. Truly, they never had a chance.

—In West Germany, stodgy public figures greeted the first showings of "Dallas" as they would a spree of acid rain. One politician labeled the show "mental chewing gum" and feared that it would breed a whole new generation of "dapper villains" like J.R. A newspaper exhorted citizens, "Write letters of protest to network editors. Then forget the Ewings!" Even *Der Spiegel,* West Germany's most prestigious publication, denounced the show: "Seldom has one seen on the television screen more inadequately constructed plots with worse actors set in more plodding scenes."

Despite the outcry, some 44 percent of the nation's viewers took the Ewings into their homes.

—"Dallas" isn't permitted on East German stations, but citizens of the Communist country still manage to view J.R. on an available network. In 1980, Mr. Ewing appeared in the flesh, and was swarmed hysterically by the East Germans.

—In Turkey, the Muslim fundamentalist National Salvation Party demanded "the elimination of 'Dallas' from television programs," charging that the show "is degrading and aims at destroying Turkish family life." On the other hand, one session of the Turkish parliament was cut short so that members could rush to their homes and turn on the latest episode.

—In Egypt, the influential Muslim fundamentalist minority finally succeeded in banning "Dallas" in 1983, citing the show's alleged obsession with wealth, greed and promiscuity. But Jordan let the show remain on its government-owned station (although it banned "Dynasty" for having a homosexual character), and in Israel, the Purim festivities now feature a new "J.R." costume.

—In Italy, restaurant owners routinely expect smaller crowds on "Dallas" nights. But the restaurant in Venice that actually discovered the infamous J.R. Ewing among its diners suddenly swelled with 3000 clawing, camera-waving fanatics.

—And in Algeria, where half of the homes have no running water and the average occupancy is

3

> eight per room, the sight of the Ewing ranch
> spellbinds the public. "No foreign production,"
> wrote a visiting journalist, "has ever had such an
> impact in Algeria."

When the outside world rails against America, it does so with symbols of American pop culture. The latest of these is Sylvester Stallone's one-man battalion, Rambo. When protestors in Munich or London or Paris select Rambo to characterize President Reagan, there's no ambivalence in the symbolism. To them, "Rambo Reagan" means America at its most evil.

And it's because of this that Rambo as a character shall be fleeting in our memory. The triumph of J.R. Ewing, on the other hand, is one of dimensionality: we hate him, we're charmed by him, we want him dead, we can't imagine life without him. J.R. is the Scrooge of the modern age—rotten almost to the core, but not quite—yet we find ourselves less likely to pity J.R. and more so to envy him.

In a fascinating *Texas Observer* article entitled "Is J.R. the Ugly American?," Pat Aufderheide explored the source of the world's appetite for "Dallas." Aufderheide concluded that "the series indulges a common love-hate attitude toward Americans" as well as "a fascination with America's vaunted wealth and power while also confirming the ancient belief that love and loyalty are destroyed by selfish powermongering."

This "powermongering" harkens back to history's yellowest pages. Clinical psychologist Harriett Moore sees "Dallas" as "a tale of classic feudalism, in which the family power broker . . . uses the family members as hostages, trade-offs and pawns in his general economic striving." But why not go back even further? One journalist, for example, described the Ewings as "the most backbiting nest of vipers since the House of Atreus was shovelled into its bloody sepulchre." And Harold Fickett of *Christianity Today* took home the blue ribbon for solemnity when he described J.R. thusly:

"He is so very attractive because he makes the fictional cosmos of 'Dallas' multi-dimensional; by his presence he lends the show the structure of Christian cosmology: heaven and earth and hell. And this is what makes the show so unusual . . ."

Granted, it seems a little ridiculous to speak of a prime-time soap opera as if it were the Old Testament. Norman Birnbaum, a Georgetown University sociologist, dismisses all the high talk about "Dallas," insisting, "Its attraction transcends national frontiers only because it adds joy to all mankind in their daily lives."

But Fickett's point is well taken. Most TV shows, he says, take place in spiritual neutrality—in the suburbs . . . abandoned, he says, "by heaven and hell to their psycho-therapists." Not so "Dallas," wherein the Ewings' Mount Olympus, Southfork, throbs with the titanic struggles between good and evil.

And in the words of Dr. Joyce Brothers, "Evil is more fascinating than good. Good only has one dimension and evil has many. At a time when we are looking for world leadership, when our world appears in chaos, we often think evil is strong, so anyone with a strong character can be appealing. People love to be fascinated with an evil that is controllable, like watching J.R. be dastardly from the safety of their living room."

But what rivets the world to J.R. Ewing is that he's not *all* bad. He is an attractive man with a boyish face ("He looks like a grown-up Beaver Cleaver and behaves like Idi Amin," snickered one TV critic), and the show's tender moments between J.R. and his son remind us that beneath the charm may lie a grain of sincerity. Having

5

INTRODUCTION

fallen from grace, we find ourselves half-hoping that the pure heart will resurface, that J.R. Ewing will find within himself a residue of decency.

So the hook of "Dallas" is a guessing game—not just whether Bobby will triumph over J.R., but also whether J.R. can demolish his own demons. The show's enthusiasts crave that added dimension of hope. But make no mistake: they could never stomach a wimpy J.R., played with horrific sensitivity by John Denver.

Instead, J.R. Ewing is played by Larry Hagman, the subject of this book. I've begun this biography with an analysis of the character rather than the actor for a reason hardly intended to slight Hagman. It may well be that he, like his good friend Carroll O'Connor, is fated forever to be dwarfed by a man of fiction.

But like Archie Bunker, J.R. Ewing will outlast Larry Hagman not simply because of reruns, but because Hagman has himself created a creature of mythological proportions. Technically speaking, Hagman didn't dream up the role of J.R.—David Jacobs gets that honor—but who can doubt that the essence of John Ross Ewing had nothing to do with scriptwriting?

Hagman is only one of several stars in "Dallas," and without some of them—Patrick Duffy, most noticeably— the show has occasionally suffered. But most people seem to think that the absence of Larry Hagman from "Dallas" would plunge the show into permanent mediocrity. And when they voice this sentiment, they aren't talking about the loss of the character, but rather the actor. There seems to be little doubt that what gives J.R. his J.R.-ness are the nuances of Hagman's invention: the bloodthirsty smile, the malevolent stare, the mock folksiness.

Larry Hagman often says that J.R.'s not such a bad guy—that he's only "protecting his family." Whether or not even Hagman believes that isn't the point. What's significant, instead, is how J.R. Ewing manages to sustain a family while continually threatening to tear it apart. Overseas, the fascination with the Ewings is more than a little reminiscent of the way people viewed the Kennedy family: as one fraught with mishaps, but nonetheless glamorous and enviable. J.R. somehow doesn't come across as the Ewings' black sheep, but rather its wicked shepherd.

One professor of psychiatric ethics, in fact, has argued that the Ewing family isn't such a bad role model. After all, he says, "they handle all their problems within the family," taking an active role in dealing with those problems. And in J.R. Ewing, one can see not only some traditional value of family, but a certain desire to help perpetuate it, in spite of himself. That sense of patriarchal control comes from Hagman—and, as will be seen in the next two chapters, from his father—not from the scripts.

In fact, the unshakable dominion of J.R. over Cliff Barnes and his other foes is a product of Hagman's conveyed sense of control. "We admire rugged individuals like Mr. Hagman's character," says anthropologist Ashley Montagu, "precisely because they can get away with it." Montagu likens J.R. to Richard Nixon, which seems dubious until you recall Nixon's "when the going gets tough, the tough get going" axiom. That's Hagman's J.R., a staunch survivalist. To borrow William Faulkner's words, he doesn't just endure—he prevails.

Faulkner, of course, never got a chance to see "Dallas." But it should already be apparent in the previous paragraphs that all sorts of people—even rather distinguished ones—find themselves talking about the Ewing family. This is partially due to the fact that as of last count, "Dallas" was being aired to an international audience of about 300 million. The thought of that is staggering: seldom has Western culture penetrated the weekly habits of distant nations so effectively.

The main source of the show's popularity, however, isn't just its global availability; rather, it's the classic themes with which "Dallas" is regularly concerned. To name a few: greed, desire, guilt, dishonesty, pride, and taste in clothes. In these respects, "Dallas" is kindred to every soap opera that ever plodded its way through American living rooms.

But Hagman's J.R. makes the difference. In terms of looks, he's no matinee idol, yet "He seems to be one of those men only a wife can resist," in the words of journalist Joseph Sobran. ("Evil is sexy," Sobran goes on to say, "until you have to pick up its socks.") J.R. may be a scoundrel, but he knows what he wants and he goes out and fetches it. Asked about the influence J.R. might have on American males, Hagman pointed out, "It's not just the coldheartedness they get out of the character, but the need for direct action. It's better than sitting around waiting for the federal government to do it to you."

And as an actor, Hagman understood the moment had come for a J.R. Ewing in the world of television. In 1980, when "Dallas" reached its astounding peak of popularity as a result of the "Who Shot J.R.?" cliff-hanger, seemingly every publication in the world buttonholed Larry Hagman and asked him, "How in the world did this show become so popular?"

And Hagman told them that television had seen too many nice guys, too many Waltons. He felt that people were ready for something a little nastier. "I think life is represented by all factions, the good and the bad," he said.

"And J.R.," Larry Hagman added, "is the bad."

But then where does that leave Larry Hagman?

The point of departure in almost everything written about Hagman is this: he's nothing like J.R. That's it. Complete opposites. No less an authority than Hagman's good friend Philip Mengel, a New York banker, has echoed this: "In real life," he said, "Larry's the exact opposite of J.R. He's a delightful, irreverent person. He's kind, a super family man but mainly a comedian who loves to have fun. He's playing a role. Nobody could be further away from J.R. than Hagman. He's my closest personal friend, was best man at my wedding. I negotiate his contracts. Believe me, I know."

Most of Mengel's words are undeniable. But it's not just on semantics that one should challenge his claim that "Nobody could be further away from J.R. than Hagman." For in truth, J.R. Ewing is, and always has been, *within* Larry Hagman. Hagman is, indeed, "playing a role"; but to play that role so effectively could not be possible without an understanding of what makes J.R. tick, what drives him. And that understanding could not be possible without the life of Larry Hagman, without the situations and conflicts that made the construction of J.R. Ewing an inevitability.

To say that J.R. Ewing resides in Larry Hagman does not make Hagman an evil man any more than temptation and inbred wickedness make any of us evil. Hagman was born in a soon-to-be-broken home, spent his formative years watching the anything-goes spectacle of oil wildcatters, and then fell into the vain and Darwinian world of acting. He had plenty of chances to become a J.R., or even worse.

That Hagman turned out, instead, to be such a spiritually positive individual constitutes his triumph over the various contrary forces. But to say that he has completely purged himself of those forces is nonsense. J.R. is who he is because Hagman is who he is: an extremely talented and complex man who has lived an interesting life that nonetheless was no easy ride.

"I love the character," Hagman once said of J.R. "He must be somewhere inside me because it comes so easy."

This book was written in the context of that fact. Not just because it's true, but because it is J.R. Ewing who has made the world curious about Larry Hagman. In a way that doesn't seem fair, since Hagman has graced the television and movie screens with his brilliance for about a quarter of a century, and honed his chops on theater stages long before that. But even Hagman would probably concede that until the first scripts of "Dallas" landed in his lap, he was on the road to becoming yet another where-are-they-now actor.

To which it should be added: hurray for those first scripts! For Larry Hagman is a remarkable man, an oddity even by Hollywood standards, and any excuse to tell his tale is greatly appreciated. Appreciated, not least of all, by the author, since spending nine months exploring the life of a television actor usually doesn't promise such great amusement.

The story of Larry Hagman is not one of dates and times, and this book hopefully reflects that. Of course, the Texas Hagman knew as a boy has changed in many ways; but as the next chapter shows, the town of Weatherford is still a sleepy one and not what you would call a metaphor of modernism. And as to whether or not a young and unestablished Larry Hagman could have made it today as a new talent, the answer is: probably. Hollywood still appreciates acting skills, recent prime-time evidence notwithstanding.

Insofar as it is possible, Hagman resembles a "man out of time." True, the young actor opposed the Vietnam War and later admitted to experimenting with drugs in the sixties and early seventies. True, the Larry Hagman of the eighties possesses a houseful of standard yuppie "toys," including video equipment and Jacuzzi. But what does a man's fondness for parading up and down Malibu Beach in a gorilla suit say of a particular era, other than the fact that it takes all kinds?

Instead, Hagman's life story is a story of people and places. Three of each are given particular coverage in this book, and in so doing, the chronology of events is from time to time disturbed. For example, chapter 1 describes Weatherford, Texas—a town in which he was not born (Hagman's birthplace is Fort Worth) and, in fact, one which meant very little to young Larry until he became a teenager.

Preceding those years with his father in Weatherford was a childhood spent more or less in the care of his mother, famed stage actress Mary Martin. That those days are chronicled in the second, rather than first chapter can be explained using the guidance of hindsight. Looking back, it now seems obvious that in the life of Larry Hagman, what made its first impact was the Texas lifestyle; following that, the career of Mary Martin. In Weatherford Larry established roots, and digested a few of life's early lessons while under his father's wing. Then he leaped into the world of his mother.

Each is given a chapter, in any event, to emphasize the persistence of their influence on Hagman, *particularly* in the context of J.R. Ewing. As many close friends as Hagman has, however, only one other individual seems to have impacted the actor significantly. That person is his wife, Maj. Much has been made of Hagman's eccentricities—and as the final chapter details, he *is* an odd bird—but perhaps the most unusual thing about him is that he has been married to the same woman for over thirty years. (And this, a TV celebrity!) In searching for Hagman's constants, Maj is clearly one of very few. She therefore merits a chapter—again, even at the risk of upsetting the flow of time.

Straddling that section are chapters 3 and 5, which attempt to lay out the chronology of Hagman's early stage and television/film careers, respectively. Most people remember Hagman as the slightly flustered astronaut playing straight-man to Barbara Eden's cleavage in "I Dream of Jeannie." But the truth is that both before and after "Jeannie," Hagman had appeared in a remarkable number of productions—though none, admittedly, of comparable success.

These were crucial years in Hagman's development, for a number of reasons. First, the fifties and sixties allowed Hagman to work with a wide variety of talented performers. Second, Hagman was given the opportunity to experiment with various dramatic forms—comedy, soap opera, drama—and to tinker with different types of roles, such as those of husband, bachelor, underling, and villain. Finally, with "I Dream of Jeannie," Hagman experienced success and the pains that accompany it.

Chapter 6 gives the account of how "Dallas" came to be, how Hagman came to be J.R., and how J.R. (and thus Hagman) came to *be* "Dallas." From the way this introduction began, it should be obvious that the author has presupposed some knowledge of the TV show on the part of the reader. Still, there is no point pretending that the interest in Hagman these days isn't largely due to "Dallas," so a discussion of the show's origins seem in order.

Until the first location shootings of the TV show, Larry Hagman had never lived in the city of Dallas. In fact, none of the cast members, producers or even writers had ever lived in the site of "Dallas." As a result, cries of inauthenticity regularly surround the show, and "foreigners" (read: non-Texans) are said to have a completely false view of this enormous and complex city.

Today, "Dallas" and Dallas enjoy a curious and ambivalent relationship, with Hagman set squarely in the middle. Hagman is the cast's only native Texan and the only star who does the state's twang justice. He also seems to be the only member of the "Dallas" club with a keen eye for what typifies modern Texas businessmen. Yet his is the role that has caused the most uproar in Dallas. Local critics claim that J.R.'s antics lead the outside world to believe that all Dallas males are conniving, adulterous oilmen with ice in their hearts and cow manure on their snakeskin boots. More than any other Texas city, Dallas loathes this particular stereotype.

Somehow, all of this has made Dallas Hagman's third home (after Malibu and Weatherford): he works there, sometimes lives there, is regarded as a native celebrity and is held accountable for his deeds there. It only seemed sensible, then, to freeze-frame the relationship between Hagman and the real Dallas, and this is done in chapter 7.

Famous people frequently are asked, "What was the turning point of your career? When did you take off and never look back?" No hemming and hawing for Hagman on this point. Larry Hagman made it big, permanently, when they shot him in front of a worldwide television audience. As is made clear in chapter 8, the story of "Who Shot J.R.?" and how it changed Larry Hagman's life isn't simply a matter of one episode and a new contract. It was, in fact, a triumph of marketing that Hagman and the show itself have never come close to repeating since.

Chapter 9 details the fallout of that triumph. Entitled

"Selling J.R.," the chapter examines the commercialization of Larry Hagman and his television show. Marketing exploitation had always been a sore spot for Hagman—at least since the days of "I Dream of Jeannie," the reruns for which he receives nary a penny. True sport that he is, Hagman has always played along with the publicity side of fame, even if it's meant typecasting himself forever. But as chapter 9 illustrates, there's only so much merchandising and marketeering a sane person can take.

Chapter 10 is called "Dateline: Malibu," but it's not just about Hagman's residency. Instead, this section deals with the more private side of Larry Hagman: his home, his family and his community ties. This is the Hagman no one sees, because Hagman himself prefers it that way.

The final chapter of this book contends that in his own way, Larry Hagman is every bit the larger-than-life character that his "Dallas" counterpart is. If there's such a thing as a disciplined hedonist, it's Hagman, who cares intensely about free-spiritedness. Would Larry Hagman trade lives with J.R. Ewing? He doesn't need to, of course: he gets to live and then abandon his character's life every few months. But would J.R. swap lives with Hagman? "Darlin'," he might reply ruefully, "I'd be crazy not to."

All of which is another way of saying that people who envy J.R. Ewing are envying the wrong man. So many actors, from Adam West to Jerry Mathers to Mary Tyler Moore, have enjoyed enormous success in a television role, only to anguish later over their inability to rid themselves of their character's image. Larry Hagman is similarly aware of the possibility that J.R. Ewing may become his albatross, preventing his audience from ever viewing him as anything other than a malicious Texas millionaire.

But as albatrosses go, it could be worse. Courtesy of

J.R., Hagman is something of an international sex symbol (something for which his wife shows remarkable tolerance); he is also very wealthy and is treated to fanfare wherever he goes.

Most of all, however, Larry Hagman *loves* J.R. Every day he lets his dastardly demon out for a few hours, then goes home a healthy man. Patrick Duffy left "Dallas" because he was sick of Bobby Ewing, and Linda Gray has warned more than once that she's tired of playing Sue Ellen Ewing, bulldozed lush. But it's hard to shake the feeling that Hagman has the time of his life playing mean ol' J.R.—again, largely because J.R. is *his*, not a scriptwriter's.

Often an interviewer will note, with some consternation, that it's hard to tell who's answering the questions, Hagman or Ewing. Several journalists refer to the almost transitionless way in which Hagman will suddenly smile devilishly, his blue eyes gleaming like Bowie knives, and make an innocent remark sound like a death sentence. Where does fact end, they wonder, and fiction begin?

That's the question this book addresses. No easy task, perhaps, but J.R. wouldn't want me piddling around with the nickels and dimes.

—Leon Adams
May 1986

CHAPTER ONE

Dateline: Weatherford

The town where Larry Martin Hagman grew up, like Mary Martin's Peter Pan, refuses to grow up.

Granted, it's doubled in population since Hagman moved away for the bright city lights in the late 1940s. But that still puts Weatherford at about 14,000 residents. Twenty miles away looms the western outskirts of the Dallas/Fort Worth Metroplex, where new hotels and condominiums clutter the once-featureless flatlands. In Weatherford, local officials got away with building a new city hall, but not without a few nasty remarks from the natives. People here didn't like the glossy "eighties" structure—said it looked out of place.

Actually, Weatherford itself would look out of place were it not for the fact that Texas is littered with other such small towns. Many, like Weatherford, are situated in "dry" counties, meaning alcoholic beverages can't be sold. Recently, it came to the attention of city officials that when Prohibition was repealed, the law stipulated that counties which had been "wet" before Prohibition would automatically return to that status. Weatherford officials aren't sure whether or not Parker County was "wet" back then—"We may be wet and not even know it," says one. Fact is, nobody's bothered to check. Obviously, Weatherford likes things the way they are.

This is, after all, the "Bible Belt," watering hole for Baptists and scourge of the liberal-minded. Some might consider Weatherford's focal point to be its magnificent old churches (many of them pre–Civil War), and it's true that many of Weatherford's social dictates originate from First Baptist and First Methodist theologies.

But the real centerpiece, quite literally, is the Parker County Courthouse, a regal old stone fortress around which Weatherford—and the entire county—was built in 1855. Larry Hagman would always regard the courthouse as the home away from home for his grandfather, his father and later, his half-brother Gary. But back in the 1850s, pioneers knew that the site of their new county seat was Indian territory. In fact, Isaac Parker, the county's founding father, was the uncle of Cynthia Anne "Quanah" Parker, who had been seized and then raised by the Comanches.

The Comanche raids ceased by 1874, and post–Civil War Weatherford immediately went about the business of agriculture. Today, only the crop has changed. At the turn of the century it had been peanuts and cotton. By the time Larry Hagman was born, the bumper crop in Weatherford was watermelon. Today it's peaches. Some vineyards can be found on the town's outskirts, as well as acreage for livestock. By all accounts, however, this is a land of the soil, and it intends to stay that way.

It is difficult to imagine a town of such modesty spawning two great talents in Larry Hagman and Mary Martin. Even today, Weatherford has but one movie theater and no museums or performing-arts venues. For a good time, people take the hour-long drive to Dallas . . . although, says Weatherford Chamber of Commerce director Perry Gott, "You see people in the obituaries every day who died in their eighties, who were born here, lived here all their lives and if the truth be known, never left the city but once or twice."

The town is quiet, but one in which there are no secrets. Even today, most Weatherford residents know each other, know who's sneaking around with whom and who's fallen off the wagon. Towns like this are gossipy and naturally suspicious of the extraordinary.

Yet both Hagman and his mother often return to Weatherford. Friends and family (most prominently, Larry's stepmother Juanita Hagman) still live here; mainly, however, it's still home. And that, at rock bottom, constitutes the appeal of sleepy old Weatherford. It's steady and predictable, with traditional schooling, hard workers and dependable neighbors. Weatherford may not be the greatest thing to look at, but it doesn't pretend to be. It's simply a good town in which to grow up—and, if one chooses, grow old—at a slow and even pace.

And if one were looking for the origin of J.R. Ewing, this would be the place to start.

William Louis Hagman looked down at his newborn son, and all he could think of were the names of his two favorite statesmen, Benjamin Franklin and Andrew Jackson. And that was that. The first inspiration for J.R. Ewing came into the world as Benjamin Jackson Hagman. It was 1908.

Tales grow in the telling, but it seems fair to say that Ben Hagman was a rather remarkable man. Ben's grandfather had been raised in Sweden, and father William had lived mainly in Wisconsin and Michigan. Ben, however, was pure Texan, tall and solid and oozing with charisma.

In Weatherford, they'll remember Ben Hagman as a freewheeling criminal attorney—a lawyer's lawyer, they say, one who would go broke fighting for a client's rights, but always within the bounds of fair play. In those days, you could make a pretty good name for yourself in Texas defending murderers and thieves, but Ben wasn't all that interested in a reputation. Mainly, he enjoyed people and wasn't the type of man who could imagine spending life behind a desk. He was a man of action, and trial law was where the action was.

"I guess he represented every criminal in town," says his widow, Juanita. And it's quite likely that Ben enjoyed rubbing elbows with the colorful characters who filtered in and out of Parker County Courthouse. Some were nothing more than habitual troublemakers, but others were of quite a different sort: high-flying, risk-taking oil wildcatters who made up rules—and broke them—as they went along.

Among Ben's oil buddies was a particularly hedonistic fellow who lived in Weatherford and had a reputation for squashing competitors like waterbugs. His idea of a good time, besides making and spending money, was to drive his jeep up the Hagmans' porch steps and leave it there for a week or two.

Remembering the wildcatter's antics, Juanita shrugs nonchalantly, as if the discussion were about the price of Weatherford pecans. "Ben didn't think a thing of it," she says. "I mean, if that's what you wanted to do, well . . ."

For young Larry Hagman, however, the wildcatter made a deep impression. One day he would serve as the model for J.R. Ewing.

*   *   *

Larry Martin Hagman stepped off the train and confronted Ben Hagman. Larry was fourteen; Ben was thirty-seven. Many years later, after Ben had been dead for over a decade, Juanita Hagman would recall flicking on the television, seeing Larry as J.R. and immediately turning the set off again. "It was back when Larry had all that extra weight on him," she says. "I couldn't bear to watch him. He looked so much like Benny . . ."

Mary Martin would also recall that when she gave birth to Larry in a Fort Worth hospital on September 21, 1931, the infant tipped the scales at eight and a half pounds. He was "the image of his father," she would write.

But in 1945, any resemblance between the two was remote. Ben was big and barrel-chested, and he wore a crew cut. Pale, slender Larry sported a pompadour.

The two were almost complete strangers. Larry's parents, Ben and Mary Martin, had divorced when the boy was five. Life since then had been a postcard existence: a whistle stop here with Mom, a few months up East in a boarding school, back to California with Grandma (Mary's mother, Juanita Presley Martin) while Mom went on the road in search of fame.

Seldom had the road led back to Weatherford. And during that time, Ben had remarried in 1939—to his legal secretary, Juanita. The newlyweds had then moved off to Europe when Ben was drafted by the 36th Division in World War II. In Europe, Juanita gave birth to a boy and named him Gary. Benjamin Jackson Hagman had his own life now, while his cosmopolitan son, Larry, truly seemed worlds away.

But the boy had a few memories of Pappy, and together with his imagination, a heroic image had been conjured up. While spending his days in a Vermont boarding school, Larry read Ernest Hemingway and Zane

Grey literature. These characters—these lusty, swaggering outdoorsmen who swilled adventure and lived off the land, they sounded just like Pappy! And from time to time, young Larry would sneak off into the woods with his BB gun, ready to tame the wilderness as he imagined his father did.

And today here they were, father looking down at son, in the Weatherford train station in 1945.

"The first thing we're going to do," said the father to the son, "is get that hair cut."

"He was such a sissy!" Juanita Hagman laughs today at the memory. "You just wouldn't believe it! He had the most beautiful hands you ever saw.

"Well, Ben decided he was gonna make a man out of Larry. And let me tell you, he did it the hard way! That poor boy had to work like a dog! Every time someone was building a house or a swimming pool, Benny would see to it that Larry had a hand in it."

Years later, Hagman would recall, "I dug latrines. I worked for Weatherford Oil Tool, making springs for oil pipes by hand while a machine right behind me did it a million times faster. I baled hay; worked a pneumatic hammer . . ."

But never did the boy say to his father, "Take this job and shove it." "Hell no!" roars Juanita. "Whatever Ben said, Larry did. And that child had blisters on top of blisters—oh, it was awful! And he was thirsty and tired. . . . But it wasn't long before he was tan."

It wasn't that Larry's grandmother in California spoiled the boy, Juanita says. But life was different in Texas: a man needed to know how to build and fix things, how to be resourceful and feed his family. Private schools weren't much at preparing kids for this sort of thing.

Ben worried, in fact, that public school life at Weatherford High—his alma mater as well as Juanita's and Mary's—might be a little rough for his son. For one thing, it wasn't really clear what grade Larry belonged in, since that matter had been lost in the endless shuffle of the sixteen schools he had attended before coming to Weatherford. So Ben brought his boy to the principal's office and said, "Put him in whatever grade you think he belongs. I'll see to it that he makes the grades."

But Ben's concern didn't stop at the books. Young Larry, after all, was the new kid in school—and one with what Juanita terms "a Yankee accent." The locals would grind him up into sawdust if something wasn't done. "Ben knew he'd get the hell beat out of him if Larry didn't get some training," says Juanita. "You know how kids are."

So Ben enrolled his son in Golden Gloves boxing. Larry's coach, as it turned out, was Jim Wright, who is the new Speaker of the House of Representatives. While not the stuff of champions, Larry learned enough to hold his own and keep the wolves at bay.

In fact, says Juanita Hagman, the day would come when Larry, having just been drafted into the Korean War, would take a look around at his brawny fellow soldiers and say, "Dad, you don't know what you did to save my life."

How was life in Weatherford in those days? It depended on what you wanted out of life. Compared to some of the surrounding towns, Weatherford was a magnet for activity. After all, there was the monthly Barter Day, a tradition since Reconstruction in which farmers from all surrounding areas came to Weatherford to trade their wares. There was also the rodeo, and the usual wedding parties and church-related activities.

But a growing boy could tire pretty quickly of that sort

of entertainment. Usually, says Gary Hagman, "We'd all just go over to Hollands Lake and throw each other in." Hollands Lake was Weatherford's designated "swimming lake": better for skiing and splashing around than fishing. For a taste of the latter, Larry and Ben would head to the Gulf Coast, or catch bass and crappie at nearby Possum Kingdom Lake.

Father and eldest son hit it off well as outdoorsmen. Besides fishing, the two would hunt for rabbits and deer, then sit back and smoke cigarettes together and "bullshit all night long," Larry would later say.

As an old friend would later say, "I don't want to give the impression that Ben was mean to his son. He may have been stern, but he was only doing it to help Larry. Believe me, he needed it!"

The family resemblance had become more apparent. In addition to loving the outdoors, Larry also enjoyed hanging around people, listening to his father talk business with his flamboyant friends and pumping Juanita for information about what it was like "in the old days."

"He sure wasn't shy," says Juanita with a chuckle. "Oh, no. Typical Hagman."

Larry got along well with his classmates, but finding his niche presented some difficulties. In Texas—particularly in the small towns, where the possibilities of social gatherings were limited—football was king. Larry tried his hand on the gridiron, but there was a slight problem: he was nearsighted and had to wear glasses. Back in the days before contact lenses and massive helmet face masks, a bespectacled football player didn't stand much of a chance.

Weatherford High, even before the days of Mary Martin, had always boasted an excellent drama department. But Larry, as is explained in the next chapter, had harbored little desire to follow in his mother's footsteps. The opportunity had always been there, but what the boy had seen so far of the acting world exhibited very little appeal to him.

Years before, Larry had made his acting debut—at a grade-school pageant, before an audience of guffawing parents. Larry had one line, but when the time came, he stared dumbly out into the crowd. So much for the acting bug.

Finally, in his senior year, Larry's desire to get involved in *something* won out. He joined the drama club, tried out for the leading role in the school play and won. In the wings of the auditorium, Larry found a publicity poster of an old Weatherford High drama production pasted to the wall. At the top of the poster were the words, "Mary Martin."

And above his mother's name, the boy wrote, "Larry Hagman."

Weatherford is a town, they say, with a "strong work ethic." But it's not the kind of town where a boy has to make career choices at an early age. In Weatherford, Larry's boyhood was spent frog-gigging or rabbit hunting at night, or driving restlessly through the quiet town streets in his jeep, or simply hanging out at the local Dairy Queen, flirting (but not getting very far) with the girls.

When asked, Larry would tell adults he might like to be a veterinarian, or maybe a circus performer—something adventurous like that. But he'd never say such a thing to Ben, who already had plans for his eldest son.

"He'd say, 'You're gonna go to the University of Texas and go to law school there and come back to Weatherford and be an attorney like me and your grandfather,'" Juanita recalls.

Certainly Larry got plenty of exposure to that sort of lifestyle. He would see his father work until three in the morning, then head back to the courthouse at eight. He would watch Ben issue pleas to the jury, then stalk around town hustling more cases.

One summer Ben took a notion to run for state senator, and took Larry with him all around the Parker County district. There Larry met all the establishment types: oil barons, cattle kings, politicians, horse traders. In a way, the tour amounted to one last opportunity for young Larry Hagman to survey all the possibilities available to him as a Texas businessman. What he saw fascinated him; later he would tell a reporter, "Let me tell you, my character is milk toast compared with some of those people. Fratricide, patricide, brothers and sisters shooting each other. It was unbelievable!"

But it wasn't the kind of life Larry Hagman could imagine living. No regrets, he had decided . . . but he wouldn't be long for Weatherford, Texas.

Today, just a few blocks down from the Parker County Courthouse, a number of fast-food franchises girdle the main street. There's a new Weatherford High, and where the old school once stood now stands the city's controversial new city hall building. A new clique has emerged in the community—the General Dynamics engineers, who have chosen to raise their family in a "wholesome" atmosphere and commute to Fort Worth every morning.

But Weatherford is still dry, and instead of advertising lounges, the city's hotels have their marquees read, "Free Coffee." The Weatherford Coffee Shop still serves a great cheeseburger for a couple of bucks, and outside the courthouse, lawyers still stand with their hands in their pockets, talking their trade in low voices.

Juanita Hagman still lives in the house Ben bought before Larry was born. A one-story white cottage on West Josephine Street, the house has seen better days and carries a faded aura. Juanita is in her seventies and isn't as adroit at household maintenance as she once was. But her son Gary, who lives just a few blocks away, comes over daily to change the light bulbs, wash the windows or fix the faucets.

Unlike his half-brother, Gary Hagman never saw much reason to leave Weatherford. His law office sits just behind the courthouse; between Gary and Ben, the Hagmans had made their mark on the city's legal affairs, since over half a century ago.

It's no secret that Gary and Larry have never been that close. They share a few physical traits—the square jaw coupled with boyish cheeks—but Gary's life is steeped in the Northwest Texas community. So, for that matter, is Juanita Hagman's life. She doesn't get out of her house that much these days, but frequently her close friends will come over and play cards, drink iced tea, smoke cigarettes and engage in some town gossip.

Juanita and Larry continue to be very close. They had their share of scuffles when Larry first came to live with Ben and his second wife, but it's obvious now that Larry regards Juanita as every bit the mother Mary Martin is to him. She occasionally flies to Malibu to stay with her stepson—"I get the room upstairs with the balcony, 'cause he won't let anyone smoke indoors," she says. During one of her visits, Larry noticed that Juanita was suffering from eye problems, at which point he whisked her off to a Los Angeles hospital and footed the bill for optical surgery.

Larry doesn't visit Weatherford quite as often as he used to, Juanita says. But when he does, he stays with her, in the same bedroom of his youth, up at the front of the house by the porch where the raucous wildcatter once parked his jeep. (Actually, when Larry became a senior, Ben and Juanita moved the teenager to the garage apartment, where he could play his records without infuriating the elders.)

"When he comes here, he doesn't want to be treated like a star," says a close friend of Juanita's. "He wants to be treated like Larry." For the most part, the town of Weatherford leaves him in peace. Occasionally Juanita's acquaintances will send over autograph requests (which is acceptable, although Larry won't sign autographs on public demand), but it's only when the family goes to another town for dinner that the mobs converge.

Usually, however, Larry eats at Juanita's—or at a neighbor's, depending on who's got the best menu for the evening. (He also washes up at the neighbor's, since Juanita's house doesn't have a shower.) In Malibu, Juanita obeys the Hagmans' nonsmoking wishes; similarly, Larry doesn't impose his dietary eccentricities on Weatherford. "He eats a lot of black-eyed peas here," says Juanita with a laugh.

Juanita faithfully watches "Dallas" and says of the man who plays J.R., "In real life, he's a teddy bear." He usually pays his visits to Weatherford while staying in Dallas for location shootings, and sometimes even brings home guests—like his "Dallas" mother, Barbara Bel Geddes. It amuses Juanita to hear Larry lapse into his J.R. dialect in mid-conversation, but usually "He sounds more like California Larry," she says.

The town of Weatherford is proud of "California Larry," but it goes on without him. Reporters frequently skulk around, digging for dirt in J.R.'s old stomping grounds. Typically, they come away empty-handed. As they soon find out, "Dallas" and Weatherford don't mix.

Says one city official, "It astounds people when I tell them, 'Not only have I not been to Southfork, but I don't watch "Dallas."' Sorry—I think Larry's a fine actor, but soap operas don't interest me.

"I think it's passé around here," says the man, unaware of the irony.

CHAPTER TWO

Son of Peter Pan

While the rest of America was celebrating the Bicentennial on July 4, 1976, the town of Weatherford had planned a different sort of festival. Today, a statue remains in front of the Weatherford Public Library to commemorate that event.

The statuesque figure is young and androgynous, with a perky, confident grin and eyes that seem to gaze keenly at some distant subject—off to the West, toward Hollywood, as it so happens. Hands on hips, legs apart, body erect, the figure is scantily attired but has the triumphant posture of a knight in shining armor.

On a plaque below the statue are the words:

PETER PAN

A TRIBUTE TO THE GENIUS
OF WEATHERFORD'S MARY MARTIN
WHO BROUGHT A MYTH TO LIFE
FOR AMERICA'S MILLIONS

SCULPTOR RONALD THOMASON
CAST BY METZ CASTLEBERRY
DEDICATED JULY 4, 1976

Encircling the statue are other smaller plaques, each bearing the title of plays the remarkable Ms. Martin immortalized: *Leave It To Me,* 1938; *One Touch of Venus,* 1943; *Lute Song,* 1946; *South Pacific,* 1949-50-51; *Peter Pan,* 1954-55; *The Sound of Music,* 1959-60-61; *I Do, I Do,* 1967. Had there been more space, dozens more could have been listed.

Today "Dallas" reaches tens of millions of households daily, numbers far in excess of those who ever had the opportunity to witness Mary Martin's magic. But when a reporter asked her what it was like to have a living legend for a son, the actress felt obliged to correct him good-naturedly.

"No, dear," she said. "*I'm* the legend—a *living* legend. 'Dallas' is a bloody cult. An American cult."

The legend was born on December 1, 1913, which happened to be Barter Day in Weatherford. In her autobiography, *My Heart Belongs,* Mary confessed that it was probably a son her parents, Juanita and Preston, were after. As it turned out, the Martins' only boy, Preston Jr., died a day after he was born. The consolation prize turned out to be Peter Pan.

Prior to the days of glory, however, little Mary was a child who refused to sit still in the languid shade of Weatherford. She was a townie, a girl who loved to wander around the Weatherford square and sneak into the Parker County Courthouse to eavesdrop on her father, a prominent attorney who eventually became a judge. When Juanita Martin drove Mary to her first kindergarten class, Mary snuck out the back door of the school and was waiting for Juanita when she returned home. This went on for several days until a compromise was reached: the teacher permitted Mary to sit in a rocking chair.

Even back then, the girl Hollywood would call "Audition Mary" craved constant motion. Ruthlessly tomboyish, young Mary Martin shattered with glee all southern belle molds. Studying was a bore; singing, dancing and reciting were the only things that kept her in school. When her mother bought her a new white dress, Mary showed her gratitude by falling off a trampoline and bleeding all over it.

Who could douse this fireball?

The young man's name was Benjamin Jackson Hagman, a sturdy Swede with two brothers and two passions: law and Mary. She was fourteen and he was nineteen when they met. Fearing that Ben would amount to yet another scholastic distraction for Mary, the Martins shipped Mary off to a ladies' finishing school called Ward Belmont in Nashville, Tennessee.

So there was sixteen-year-old Mary Martin in Nashville, away from her man and her parents, stifled by the rigidities of the private school and showing the usual signs of restlessness. To the rescue came her mother and Ben by car one weekend—ostensibly for a visit, but that's not quite how things turned out.

Ben asked Mary if she would marry him. She said yes. The two then persuaded Juanita to give her legal consent. To Mary's amazement (and eventual chagrin), the mother gave her blessings. So the three of them drove to Hopkinsville, Kentucky—where it didn't matter how old the bride happened to be—and picked up a marriage license, then conducted an ad hoc ceremony in an Episcopal church.

Whereupon the three drove all the way back to the gates of Ward Manor. Mary kissed her new husband and her mother and went back to school. The flippancy of it all was not lost on her later.

It wasn't long before seventeen-year-old Mary found herself pregnant, and then giving birth to Larry. The new mother adored her boy, but couldn't shake the feeling that he seemed more like a little brother and Ben her big brother. Anyway, the maternal life didn't sit well with her. It required, after all, an enormous sum of idle hours while Ben went out hunting with his pals or studied for the bar exams in Austin. Mary was back living with her parents in those days, and Larry was usually looked after by Juanita—for everyone's sake, since, as Mary would later write, the boy seemed to suffer an endless string of accidents under her care.

At her sister Billie's suggestion, Mary decided to make use of her free time teaching dance. She selected an old grain-storage room as her studio—a room, in fact, that today stands empty, although a construction firm has taken over the building—and spread the word. At first, disapproving rumbles could be heard, since dancing in the Bible Belt in those days was deemed a sinful practice. But when Mary began to travel to other areas—first Fort Worth, then Hollywood—to learn new steps, her reputation grew.

One day Mary wandered into an audition by accident, won, and found herself dancing in San Francisco. Then came an offer to sing in Los Angeles. By this time, her burgeoning dance classes had caused her to open two new schools, in the nearby towns of Cisco and Mineral Wells. Business was good, but it was small change compared to what now stood before her.

For the last five years, Mary had been questioning herself for not enjoying the married life with Ben. He was a kind, hard-working, fun-loving man, but the role Mary had assumed just didn't fit her ambitions. It was time, she decided, to face facts. Marriage had been a mistake, and a far better fate loomed on the horizon.

So Mary said goodbye to Ben, moved to Hollywood and took five-year-old Larry with her. The year was 1936.

Larry Hagman would later insist that the years 1936-1945 were really quite pleasant. Certainly they were educational: at this tender age, Larry saw more of the United States than almost every graybeard in Weatherford.

Mary spent most of her time plowing through auditions. Because of the demanding hours, she was often asleep while Larry prowled around the house. When together, the two gabbed like buddies rather than mother and son. She nicknamed him "Luke," and he in turn dubbed her "Mimi."

Suddenly striking it rich on the Hollywood nightclub circuit, Mary felt wealthy enough to send Larry off to military school in Los Angeles. Larry hated it and longed for the great outdoors of Texas, but at the time Mary worried that the absence of a father figure would take its toll on the boy. When Larry complained, Mary would simply transfer him from one private school to another.

In 1939, while Ben Hagman and his new wife were adjusting to life in wartime Europe, Mary Martin was crooning "Daddy" in the Broadway smash *Leave It To Me*. One night after a performance, Mary was met offstage by one of her fellow performers, who informed her that her real daddy, Preston, had just died following a cerebral stroke.

Shortly thereafter, Juanita Martin, Mary's mother, moved to Hollywood and immediately resumed the care of Larry. This suited the boy just fine, since the two had gotten along famously in Weatherford. And with his father overseas and his ambitious mother's career in high gear, Larry could once again feel a reassuring sense of family.

This became particularly important by 1940, when Mary became involved with and subsequently married Hollywood director Richard Halliday. The new man in Larry's life seemed, in the boy's eyes, to be a completely unsuitable substitute for his strapping Texas father. A brilliant and worldly man, Halliday nonetheless clashed with the macho image Larry preferred. The Hollywood executive's attempts to appease the fiery lad fell flat.

In 1942, Mary and Halliday gave birth to a baby girl, Heller, and then headed off to Broadway while Larry stayed in Hollywood with Juanita Martin. Two years later, Larry's sole source of family stability caved in when Juanita died suddenly from a stroke.

Mary and Halliday brought Larry back to their Manhattan apartment. When that arrangement didn't work out, Larry found himself staying with Halliday's mother near the Connecticut Berkshires. Finally, Mary delivered her son to Vermont and yet another military institute— "the best place to send boys for discipline in the 1940s," Larry later said, while adding that discipline wasn't necessarily what he lacked.

What Larry Hagman lacked was a mother and a father. A year later, father and son reunited at the Weatherford train station. It took a little longer for Larry to link up with Mary.

"I often have felt that I cheated my children a little," wrote Mary. "I was never so totally *theirs* as most mothers are. I gave to audiences what belonged to my children, got back from audiences the love my children longed to give to me."

Her son is a little less candid on the subject. Today,

LARRY HAGMAN

Larry refuses to talk about whatever animosity he felt for his mother during his adolescence. The press has blown their chilly phases out of proportion, and those days have long since passed. In fact, Larry's reluctance to talk to the media these days stems partially from insinuations certain tabloids have made about the continuing turbulence of their mother-son dealings.

"We have a very nice relationship," he has said, "the best it's ever been. I find she's matured a lot over the years, and is able to handle my idiosyncrasies." Some of those idiosyncrasies—like Larry's fetish for costumes—came from Mary, she now speculates. That talent runs in the family is a great source of pride to her—even if it's Larry the public first recognizes.

More than once, the two have discussed the possibility of Mary appearing on "Dallas," although nothing's come of it yet. In the meantime, they have considered a different sort of collaboration. Since Mary began her career in Hollywood on the nightclub circuit, it only seems fitting that she be able to conclude her career in a bar, sitting on a piano and singing. Larry has said that he would like nothing better than to build a small bar into the Stanford Court Hotel in San Francisco, where his mother could do two shows a night, five nights a week for audiences of about eighty.

And, of course, there would be special guests . . . such as Larry himself, who once sang "Get Out Those Old Records" with his mother on an album for Columbia Records. That project, incidentally, netted Larry a whopping royalty check totalling exactly three cents.

At the age of fourteen, Larry got an unusual offer from his mother. Mary was going on the road with *Annie Get Your Gun,* and invited Larry to take the tour with her.

Larry declined, not wanting "to be hanging out with a bunch of sissies."

A year later, Mary again dangled in front of her son what she thought to be another tempting travel offer. This time the destination was London, accompanied by Mary, Halliday and Heller, to see Noel Coward. Upon learning that his cowboy boots would not be acceptable at their temporary residence—the uptown Savoy Hotel—Larry again refused.

Twice spurned, Mary made no other such offers. Larry stayed in Weatherford with his fishing rods and his guns.

But at the age of seventeen, Larry succumbed to the Weatherford High drama instructor's request and starred in his first high-school production. The result took him completely by surprise: he was a hit, and smitten overnight with the sensation of the stage.

That summer, Larry got a job baling hay on a Weatherford farm. He saved all the money, then bought a Greyhound ticket and headed east for Connecticut.

Upon arrival, son confronted mother, giving her the most delightful surprise of her life.

"Mother," he announced, "I think I made a mistake. I like the theater."

CHAPTER THREE

On Becoming a Struggling Actor

Telling Mary he wanted to act was one thing. Telling Ben he didn't want to be a lawyer was quite another.

When Larry graduated from Weatherford High, his father offered to pay his way to the University of Texas. Larry knew what that meant: a pre-law major, then on to law school and back to Weatherford to follow in the family tradition. Then came the graduation-present offer from Mary: either a new car, or a plane ticket to Europe. In the old days, the car might have won out. Secure in his decision to become an actor, however, Larry concluded that what he really needed was to broaden his experience. He took the ticket.

Before leaving, Larry took his stepmother, Juanita Hagman, aside. "Mother," he told her, "you wait 'til I'm in the middle of that ocean before you tell Dad: I'm not coming back. I'm going to acting school."

"It nearly broke his heart," Juanita now says. "I waited three or four days after Larry left, and then I had to tell him. Man, was he sick! He wanted *so* much for Larry to become a lawyer . . ."

But the die was cast. Larry kicked around Sweden for two months, experienced life beyond Weatherford, and then returned to the States and enrolled in Bard College in New York. Larry's grades weren't much, but having a famous and wealthy mother helped influence the admissions department.

Once accepted, however, Larry reverted to his undisciplined studying habits. Part of the problem was that he selected theater as his major, but spent most of his time building sets and designing costumes. That kind of tedium wasn't exactly what the young man had in mind. It became clear that if Larry Hagman was going to develop his skills as an actor, he wasn't going to do so in acting school.

Facing facts, he dropped out of Bard in 1949 and headed south. His inauspicious beginning as a professional actor found him, ironically, in Dallas—at the Margo Jones Theater in the Round. The play was *Romeo and Juliet,* and Larry's part required that he carry a spear and otherwise blend in with the stage props.

Back to New York went Larry in 1950, and immediately he found work—in straw-hat musicals. Not yet twenty years old, the young actor spent the next several months singing and dancing his way across New Jersey in a stint of about fifty productions.

While Larry was searching for an artistic toehold, his mother Mary had made the stroll to easy street. She had taken Broadway by storm as the "Daddy" girl in *Leave It To Me;* for an encore, she starred in eleven consecutive forgettable Hollywood films, but then returned to the stage and picked up right where she had left off. In 1943 *A Touch of Venus* premiered, with Mary Martin starring in place of Marlene Dietrich, for whom the production had originally been intended. *A Touch of Venus* ran on Broadway for 567 performances and catapulted Mary to stardom.

Other critical and commercial successes followed, but the one that counts forever in the hearts of millions is the unforgettable *Peter Pan.* For three years—1954 in San Francisco and Los Angeles, 1955 on Broadway and national television, and 1960 for a final television performance—Mary Martin personified the joy and freedom of he who swore to "never grow up." It was a role that never ended for Mary: not offstage, where she waited for every child to leave the theater before changing herself from Peter back into the actress; and not in public, where people to this day gush their effusive memories and imitate Peter Pan's exuberant crowing.

So uplifted, in fact, were those fortunate enough to see Mary's performance that a journalist felt compelled to ask Larry Hagman many years later, "How can J.R. Ewing possibly be the son of Peter Pan?"

The man with the wicked grin knew the correct reply, naturally. Said Larry Hagman, "Peter Pan carried a knife."

In the years that followed this surge to immortality, the actress would suffer more than her share of heartaches. After an intensely loyal thirty-three-year marriage, her beloved Richard Halliday died of pneumonia in 1973. Subsequently she drew into herself and into the care of her manager, Ben Washer. But on September of 1982, a van barreled through a red light and struck a taxi that contained Mary, Ben, and her closest friend, Janet Gaynor. Washer was killed, and Gaynor seriously injured. (Two years later, Gaynor also died.)

During her long convalescence in the San Francisco hospital, Mary's most frequent companion was her son Larry, who commuted between the studio and the hospital for many days. The visits served as stirring testimony to the evolution of their friendship; in truth, however, the boy who shunned the "sissies" in Mary's life for the hard-edged life of Texas had long since eaten his words.

In autumn of 1951, *South Pacific*—based on James Michener's *Tales of the South Pacific*—opened at the Drury Lane Theatre Royal in London. Mary Martin starred as Nurse Nellie Forbush and played to standing-room-only audiences. Among those standing was her son Larry, who had elected to wait in line for hours rather than ask Richard Halliday for freebies.

As a struggling actor in New York, Larry had been receiving fifty dollars a week for three months from his mother, "to get started." But *South Pacific* offered him the chance to make his money on his own. This time Larry took the offer, joining the cast as a Seabee and enjoying a brief scene on the same stage as his mother.

It wasn't instant fame, but you couldn't argue with the exposure—or the pay, which was twelve pounds a week, a sizable sum in those days. Larry stayed with *South Pacific* for over a year. While Mary Martin often insists that her son "made it on his own," Larry candidly admits that during those years he rode his mother's long coattails. And after all, why not? His half-sister, Heller, had played Liza the maid alongside her mother in *Peter Pan,* and when Larry lodged his decision, there didn't seem much point in pretending that the name Mary Martin wouldn't help take him places.

There would be plenty of chances to rise or fall strictly on his own merits.

Back home in Weatherford, Ben Hagman had adjusted to his eldest son's elected vocation. Whenever possible, Larry later said, Ben would also try to see his ex-wife perform—"Dad would go to all her opening nights and cry his eyes out," he said. The split had never caused any animosity between Ben and Mary; in fact, Ben's new wife, Juanita, became fast friends with Mary, and today they remain on very close terms.

But for now, Larry's mind was far away from the small town. It would be over a quarter-century later before the actor would once again find himself wearing cowboy boots.

For now, Larry had fallen in love with London and didn't want to leave it. He was making good money, getting great stage experience and having fun dating hordes of British women. The latter was of particular interest to Larry, since the no-dancing atmosphere of the Texas Bible Belt hadn't been very conducive to sex education . . . nor, for that matter, had the various military institutes and boarding schools prepared him for dating.

At the outbreak of the Korean War, Larry suspected his number would come up, but wanted to stay right where he was. He enlisted in the air force as an expatriate, and as a result was penalized an extra year of service for being stationed in Europe.

Four years in the air force might have been excruciating—even with the Golden Gloves preparation—so Larry enlisted with the stipulation that he be kept away from the front lines. "I didn't want to get my ass shot off in Korea," he later said. "I'm no dummy."

Instead, Corporal Larry Hagman landed one of the cushiest jobs in the air force. For four years, he produced and directed service shows not only in England, but throughout Europe. Oh, what a lovely war.

"I had my own empire," Hagman would later recall. "A major, two lieutenants, four sergeants, all working for me—and I was only a shitfire corporal, a two-striper. I booked all the NCO clubs, a very important position in the war against communism."

The fateful plane ticket to Europe had indeed paid off. At the tender age of twenty-one, Larry Hagman had already galloped through over fifty musicals, and had managed to support himself as a stage actor by appearing in an internationally acclaimed musical. And now, the coup of coups! While the futures of other young men were being postponed or forever dismantled by the Korean War, Larry Hagman had found a way to serve his country, support himself, accumulate more theater experience and travel through Europe, all at the same time!

The hard road for the young man from Weatherford was far from finished. But for now, he had a right to feel pretty smug. He had just pulled off a scam that would leave a certain dastardly oilman from Texas feeling downright envious.

CHAPTER FOUR

Maj

J.R. Ewing notwithstanding, Larry Hagman has never been anything less than a liberated male. He grew up, after all, in an atmosphere dominated by women, and one in which money and stature were provided by his mother. Journalists have often questioned whether or not Larry's environment had been "stable," and certainly there must be easier ways to live than plodding from one boarding school to another, or, when home, finding your mother still asleep in the afternoon, exhausted from late-night performances. But what Larry learned from the experience is that women—even mothers—have just as much right to make a career for themselves as men do.

So no mandate for hitching up with a typical Southern-belle high-waisted homemaker ever really seized Larry. At the same time, acting is a profession for brooding ego-centrics, for people who not only must warp their own personalities for a living, but who also come to depend on public affection. The best partnerships between actor and mate seem to be those in which the mate possesses enormous patience, tolerance and sensitivity. Such was the case between Mary Martin and Richard Halliday. And such is still the case between Larry Hagman and his leading lady.

While battling rampant communism as a director of service shows for the air force, Larry lived in England with a close friend, British writer Henry Kleinman. Both were bachelors and dated quite extensively. By this time, Larry had "filled out," as his stepmother Juanita recalls. "He had just shot up several inches, and he didn't look so frail anymore," she says. "The first time he came home to visit, he looked so gorgeous in his uniform—like a man!"

Larry had become quite handsome, and along with his status as an actor and corporal, managed to snare a few women. He would later theorize that "after two years, English manhood had been absolutely decimated. They didn't have enough to go around." Duty called, of course.

One night, Henry Kleinman brought home a young woman for tea. She was Maj Axelsson, a twenty-five-year-old designer from Sweden. True to her origin, she had a sturdy, confident frame, blue eyes and extremely blond hair.

Her first impression of Larry Hagman was not particularly favorable. That night, a yellow motor scooter buzzed up to the front door, and in stepped Corporal Hagman, carrying bottles of gin and whiskey and sacks of food from the air force supply station. In the eyes of the Swede, he looked for all the world like the stereotypically smug and oblivious G.I. Joe.

"Well, food was very scarce, you know," she would later say. "And here was this fancy American who flaunted everything. I thought he was overpaid."

But Maj (pronounced "my") caught Larry's eye, and he decided then and there to woo her. Actually, young Hagman turned out to be far removed from the Ugly American

Maj had mistaken him for. Thanks largely to his mother, he was well traveled and had accumulated a fascinating cultural sensibility, for someone who began his life in a town like Weatherford. Larry had always enjoyed music, including jazz and baroque, and that rather impressed Maj.

"I had been led to believe that Americans were very shallow in culture compared to the Europeans, but Larry was way out ahead of any of us," she said.

The two began to date steadily. Just a few weeks after they had met, Larry and Maj borrowed a car to attend a service show Larry had produced, only to get stuck in a mud field. "We were up to our hubcaps in mud, couldn't go anywhere," said Hagman later, "and while we waited for a farmer's tractor to pull us out, I said, 'I hadn't planned to do it this way, Maj, but will you marry me?'

"She said, 'Sure, okay.'"

The following day, Larry reported to his commanding officer and filled out forms requesting permission to marry. The officer studied the forms; the woman's name, it said, was Maj Irene Axelsson. Back came the forms: Permission Denied. An enlisted man, it was explained, could not marry a major.

Explanations were made, and on September 21st, 1954, they were wed in a Swedish ceremony at a Lutheran church. It was Larry's twenty-third birthday.

The Hagmans spent two more years in Europe while Larry finished his tour of service. They weren't quite sure what to do after that. Already Maj had visited Texas and could not quite imagine living in that sort of environment.

"There's a kind of madness that prevails," she said, recalling her first visit. "People do nothing but talk about oil as if you could wear it or live in it or have it for supper. Always there was the oil strike, the big one due to come any minute."

A stopgap measure came courtesy of Mary and Richard Halliday. Mary was touring the country following the "Peter Pan" television performances, and offered Larry and Maj their Brazilian farm.

But life away from the stage "didn't suit me," Larry later said, adding, "You had to learn another language." Taking stock of this, the Hagmans headed for Manhattan. For the ensuing decade or so, they lived in a fifth-floor walk-up apartment on West Forty-ninth Street, paying $126 a month for rent.

Within a few short years, the Hagman family had grown to four. The first was a girl, whom Larry and Maj named Heidi—at the suggestion of Mary, who thought the name sounded appropriately Swedish as well as suitably catchy to be emblazoned on a theater marquee. Next came Preston, named after Mary's father.

By degrees, the West Forty-ninth Street apartment accommodated itself to the new residents. Maj applied her decorating skills to what at first looked like a tenement dwelling, by knocking out walls and giving the place an open, spacious look.

While Maj tore things down at home, Larry combed the streets looking for acting work. As it turned out, the problem wasn't finding roles, but rather getting the outside world to notice. He got his Broadway debut in *Comes a Day,* which also launched the career of George C. Scott. Later came *The Nervous Set* and *The Warm Peninsula,* as well as *God and Kate Murphy*—the latter directed by future Malibu next-door neighbor Burgess Meredith and stage-managed by eventual close friend Carroll O'Connor of Archie Bunker fame.

Four Broadway shows in one year—but all died at the box office. No longer under the wing of his famous mother, Larry Hagman was on his own. And with a family to support. And hurting for money.

CHAPTER FIVE

"Jeannie" and Lesser Triumphs

Both on and off-Broadway, success seemed destined to elude Larry Hagman. After years of comfortable living when the pressure was off, he now had a wife and two children to support—and a bundle of debts mounting.

Finally, Larry got lucky. In an off-Broadway production of *Career* by Jimmy Lee, Larry was cast in a tiny role—that of a drunk Texas soldier. The play itself was very somber, concentrating on the anguish of a man who had been blackballed in the McCarthy era. In that context, Larry embodied a most welcome comic relief and stole the show.

As a direct result, Larry Hagman received his first offers from what would become his entertainment vehicle of choice: television. The initial stints weren't much—mainly spot appearances in live television, such as the "The Alcoa Hour" and the "Armstrong Circle Theater"—but they amounted to the smoothest possible transition from the stage. And, of course, Larry was grateful for anything that paid well.

Those gigs, in turn, led to two and one-half years as a young husband embroiled in the popular histrionics of "The Edge of Night." Those days seem rather insignificant now, overshadowed as they are by the higher glamour of "Dallas." But for a young actor, "The Edge of Night" constituted an important break. Beyond the steady work and handsome pay, the soap opera enjoyed immense popularity during Larry's years there (1962–65). It seemed likely that if the show's appeal could be sustained, someone in the industry would be bound to notice.

Someone did, but before that could happen, Larry went back to Broadway for one more commercial disaster. The play was S.J. Perelman's *The Beauty Part*, starring Bert Lahr. It seemed to have everything going for it except its timing: *The Beauty Part* opened on December 1962, during New York City's sixteen-week newspaper strike. The result might well answer the question, "If a tree falls in a forest and no one is around to hear it, does it make a sound?"

Then came the genie. The one named Jeannie, that is.

The treatment for the television situation comedy "I Dream of Jeannie" called for a dizzy-headed bombshell and an all-American astronaut with a dash of playboy in him. When the offer fell in Larry's lap, he had little doubt that he could make the astronaut, Major Anthony Nelson, come to life. "I was ready for the character and the character was ready for me," he later said. "Getting breaks is only half of it. You've got to be ready." Back it was to Hollywood for Larry Hagman and his family.

In concocting an implausible sitcom plot line, the creators had outdone themselves with "I Dream of Jeannie." The series would involve the continuing misadventures of bachelor Nelson with genie Jeannie, whom the former

47

had literally uncorked from—what else—a stray genie bottle.

Like most genies, Jeannie would have the capability to make Nelson's wishes come true ... but being of a slightly airheaded nature, Jeannie's knack for misapplying her powers would lead to all sorts of uncomfortable predicaments for the nerve-wracked astronaut. Not wanting to dispense with his beautiful genie (but also not wanting to shack up with her, for reasons the sitcom never made clear), Major Nelson would struggle continually with the flip side: how to keep Jeannie's presence concealed from the outside world—particularly from his dour superior.

From time to time, the show actually dealt with the moral dilemma of "Master" Nelson's desires (and Jeannie's instant ability to fulfill them) versus his ingrained work ethic. Also implicit, due to Nelson's continual dating in the presence of his gorgeous genie, was the notion that "the perfect woman" wasn't everything.

For the most part, however, "I Dream of Jeannie" amounted to good airheaded entertainment. As a character, Jeannie followed on the heels of Samantha the humanoid witch in "Bewitched," with Nelson a conceptual dead ringer for Samantha's eternally befuddled husband, Daron. Such shows, along with "The Addams Family" and "The Munsters," followed the anything-but-human-protagonist formula for which the less imaginative "My Mother the Car" and "Mr. Ed" had been the prototype.

These were the mid-sixties, after all, when consensus was dissolving in the midst of racial tensions, the advent of the generation gap and the acceleration of the Vietnam War. Even sitcoms required conflict, and perhaps the gentlest way to introduce it in such uneasy times was through a not-quite-human species. People bickering with people wasn't funny anymore, but an astronaut chasing a genie back into her bottle might have seemed a bit more innocuous.

Whatever the cause, "I Dream of Jeannie" became a hit the day it premiered, in the fall of 1965. Like the best sitcoms, "Jeannie" enjoyed a nice balance of characters: the bubbly genie, the fretting astronaut, his relentlessly silly friend Captain Roger Healy (played to perfection by Bill Daly, who would play essentially the same character on "The Bob Newhart Show") and the terminally stoic Colonel Alfred Bellows (played by Hayden Rorke). Unlike today's ensemble casts, the scripts of "Jeannie" always focused on these four central characters, plus one or two guests who would somehow get caught up in Jeannie's hijinks. Following this format, story lines were more predictable, but also tighter and more prone to resolution.

The stars, of course, were Major Anthony Nelson and Jeannie—played by Hagman and Barbara Eden. Eden was not what one would call a veteran actress, but for the part of Jeannie she was perfect: oozing with both innocence and sensuality, daffy while at the same time hinting of a mystical knowledge. And if her squealing refrain of "Oooh, *Master*!" grated occasionally, her sex appeal—enhanced by what at that time was clearly television's skimpiest wardrobe—never did.

And could there be any doubt that Larry Hagman *was* Major Nelson? In almost other-worldly contrast to J.R. Ewing, Larry's astronaut was stammering, vulnerable, both professionally and sexually repressed, and a gentleman to the core. The astronaut label, of course, had very little to do with the character beyond underscoring his right-stuff stature; but with his tall, sturdy frame and his boyish yet attentive face, Larry Hagman was every American's image of what our men in outer space should be like.

LARRY HAGMAN

Larry Hagman was a star. The show paid him $150,000 a year and afforded him instant visibility. The day would come when the thought of "I Dream of Jeannie" would infuriate Larry, since he would never see a penny from the reruns; but for now, the thirty-four-year-old actor had proved himself when it counted—without the help of his mother, who delighted in her son's success.

Ben Hagman, unfortunately, did not live long enough to see the show. Shortly after the "Jeannie" pilot was taped, Larry phoned his Weatherford parents, promising to bring by a copy. But one thing led to another, and by the time a copy of the premiere was made available in 1965, the rugged trial lawyer from Northeast Texas had called it a lifetime.

The notion of an outdoorsman like Ben hunkering down in front of a television to watch his son sternly lecture a female genie might seem a little dubious. But the lawyer's warmth toward Larry had never changed, and he had followed his eldest son's career with great pride, knowing that Larry had displayed the stubborn individualism Juanita would term "typical Hagman." And a Weatherford neighbor remembers Ben visiting her husband in the hospital every afternoon, just in time to catch his son on "The Edge of Night."

The same neighbor remembers Larry in the days of "Jeannie"—"He seemed as happy as he could be," she recalls. But things weren't a bed of roses for the new television star. Larry had always been a fighter, striving to improve not only his own performances, but the performances of other people involved in his productions. Now, having reached his highest plateau, he had run out of yearnings. The road to becoming had suddenly ended—he was *there*. And Larry was not entirely prepared for the sensation.

There were other problems. Larry and Barbara Eden never brawled, but it was hard not to feel any resentment toward their respective situations. Major Nelson, after all, had to be on camera during some 80 percent of the scenes, and his role required the most work, since the dimensionality of the show couldn't be expected from the role of Jeannie. But Barbara Eden was the star, the glamour girl, and Larry Hagman essentially played straight man to her antics. It wasn't easy.

Then there was the small matter of the person who played an astronaut publicly denouncing the Vietnam War. As Hagman would later recall, many of his media friends were so astounded by his outspokenness on this subject that they refused to print his views. The "Jeannie" producers simply told him to keep his mouth shut.

By the end of the first season, Larry Hagman was ready to fall apart. As he would later describe in unsettling detail to the media, the pressures built up to the extent that he became nauseous on a daily basis. "I was screaming and yelling, vomiting and crying," he later told a reporter. "It was nervous breakdown time. Oh God, I even spanked my little boy on his butt, I was so far gone."

Seeing no other alternative, both he and Maj—on whom Larry's turbulence also took its toll—began to see a psychoanalyst. Larry would later report that upon hearing the actor's tribulations, the psychoanalyst offered this advice: "Don't worry. Be happy."

Those simple words impacted Larry enormously. To this day, a small sign on his bathroom mirror echoes those words, along with Larry's personal addition: "Feel good."

To supplement his therapy, Larry also took up meditation and studied Zen and Tao. Already, the idiosyncrasies that would one day make Larry the talk of Malibu, California were rising to the surface. On the "Jeannie" set, for example, the actor was fond of showing up in a train conductor's uniform or in full Indian regalia. Yet they also saw his private side every day around lunchtime, when his wife, Maj, would dutifully bring him his lunch in the studio.

"I felt then that he was a very shy fellow who could only come out of himself by doing those crazy things," said Bob Palmer, a studio executive who knew Hagman in those days. "And he didn't want to be ignored, because being ignored is the worst thing that can happen to an actor."

By the end of the sixties, the audience's love affair with "I Dream of Jeannie" had worn thin. The dwindling ratings weren't indicative of anything other than the typically short-lived value of sitcoms, particularly of the alien-protagonist genre. Within a couple of years, situation comedies would return to the family conflicts popularized by "The Dick Van Dyke Show" and "I Love Lucy," only with a greater willingness to nose around the stickier issues of sex, women's rights and racism. "The Mary Tyler Moore Show" and "All in the Family" would leave "I Dream of Jeannie" and "Bewitched" in a cloud of anonymity.

Larry Hagman's portrayal of Major Anthony Nelson, and thus his bout with celebrity, ended in 1970. "I Dream of Jeannie" was stuffed back in its bottle and tossed into the abyss of forgotten sitcoms.

Before, during and after "Jeannie," however, Larry Hagman had tested different waters: Hollywood. It might astonish even the most die-hard Hagman aficionados to learn that between 1964 and 1982, the television star acted in over fifteen major motion pictures; that he played alongside cinema legends like John Wayne, Walter Matthau and Ruth Gordon; and that his roles have ranged from a heartless high-school football coach to a sleazy Hollywood agent.

Larry began his part-time movie career in 1964 with a surprisingly major role: as the president's interpreter in *Fail Safe,* the harrowing speculative account of a nuclear accident that is at least fifteen years ahead of its time. In the movie, Hagman wears horn-rimmed glasses and fidgets deferentially to the president, played by Henry Fonda.

That same year saw the release of *Ensign Pulver,* an unfortunate attempt to sequelize *Mister Roberts.* Few saw the movie, but had they bothered, they might have witnessed the promising talents of two budding actors in minor roles: Hagman and a fellow named Jack Nicholson.

In 1965, two Hagman movies again reached the public. Like *Ensign Pulver* and the musical *South Pacific,* Larry again found himself in a naval production, *In Harm's Way*—a war story loaded with talent (John Wayne, Henry Fonda, Kirk Douglas, Paula Prentiss and Hagman's pal Carroll O'Connor), but not much else. In a similar vein, Hagman played a World War II soldier trapped in a German munitions dump with a gorgeous woman and five other soldiers in *The Cavern.*

The following year reversed the male-female ratio with *The Group,* wherein Larry found himself surrounded by Vassar graduates. Shortly after the end of the road with "Jeannie," Hagman returned to movies with *Up in the Cellar* (later retitled *Three in the Cellar* to ride the coattail of *Three in the Attic*), notable for Hagman's mustache and his co-star: Joan Collins, the "Dynasty" counterpoint to J.R. Ewing.

On a lark, Hagman both directed and starred in 1972's *Beware! The Blob*—later rereleased and subtitled, for qualitative reasons, *The Movie J.R. Shot.* Two years later, however, Larry finally participated in an outstanding, affectionate movie called *Harry and Tonto*. Starring Art Carney and Ellen Burstyn, the movie deals with the isolation of the elderly, with soft touch and a fine sense of humor. Hagman, playing Carney's self-pitying son-in-law, stands out in his supporting role.

Then followed *Stardust* in 1974, a curious movie made in the U.K. about the pitfalls of rock 'n' roll stardom. Satirically poignant, the movie has an additional merit: it features Hagman as a scumbag-type manager Porter Lee Austin, a J.R. prototype complete with Texas accent.

Five other roles followed in the seventies: a doctor in a disaster-movie parody, Gary Busey's football coach, an oversexed ambulance driver opposite Raquel Welch, an auto-race promoter and yet another military role in *The Eagle Has Landed,* a brilliant 1976 release that starred Michael Caine, Donald Sutherland and Robert Duvall.

As a supplement to "Dallas," Hagman would also star as a CBS executive in Blake Edwards' *S.O.B.* and as a helicopter pilot in the television movie "The Deadly Encounter." But as the actor had already learned, role competition in the movies was almost suffocating. Working with screen legends had its own rewards, but Larry Hagman wasn't interested in living in another star's shadow. Clearly, television was his niche.

So Hagman searched for another sitcom vehicle. After "Jeannie," the first pilot in which he performed was "The Good Life," in 1971, in which Hagman's character and his newly married wife would forestall careers and instead go into domestic service for a rich man. "The Good Life" never got off the ground, so Hagman tried again in 1973. This time it was "Here We Go Again," an inane sitcom about newlyweds whose respective ex-mates happen to be neighbors. Like "The Good Life," "Here We Go Again" plunged during its first year.

Between the pilots and his movie work, Larry continued to pull in around $150,000 annually. But once again, he felt stuck. Like Adam West of "Batman," TV producers seemed reluctant to believe that Larry was versatile enough to take on a role that didn't involve a voluptuous genie. Progress again seemed elusive.

But Larry Hagman wouldn't give up. Somewhere out there was a script. . . .

CHAPTER SIX

A Cad Is Born

For eighteen months, Larry Hagman couldn't find a job in Hollywood. Finally, Lorimar Productions sent him a package containing two scripts for two different prospective television series. The first one represented the pilot for "The Waverly Wonders"; Hagman didn't think much of the idea and passed on it. Lorimar eventually gave the lead to ex-quarterback Joe Namath, after which "The Waverly Wonders" rolled over and died a premature death.

As for the second script . . .

After years of writing children's books and short stories in New York, David Jacobs packed his bags and headed west for Hollywood in 1976. "I figured I could write TV scripts to finance my serious work, just as I had done ghost writing and freelance editing to finance my stories and novels," he said.

In his attempt to find steady work, Jacobs got his first shot writing scripts for "The Blue Knight," a police drama that unfortunately saw cancellation after a mere four weeks. The writer fared better with his next project, "Family," which launched the career of Kristy McNichols. As story editor for "Family," Jacobs made connection with CBS director of drama development Richard Burger, and the two began to contemplate various new projects.

Jacobs had always been fond of "Scenes from a Marriage," Ingmar Bergman's British TV miniseries starring Liv Ullman. He suggested to Burger a similar sort of series, "but with four families instead of one, and done in the style of American television: fast-paced and entertaining," Jacobs later said. Burger liked the idea, and eventually used it—for "Knots Landing." For now, however, the CBS executive suggested that Jacobs toss out the West Coast nuances in his story line and "try something rich and Southwestern instead of something middle class and Californian."

Said David Jacobs, "I went home and wrote a letter to myself about this terribly good-looking, semi-trashy lady who marries into a rich Texas family." The woman, Pamela Barnes Ewing, would discard her questionable past and assert herself as the show's heroine.

But Jacobs knew that wasn't enough. "Then I had to write a family," he said. "Before I had even got to the script, we had complicated things too much. We had created a ranch hand who had brought her out to the barbecue where she met Bobby (Ewing). We had decided that the family's father was once partners with her father. And so on. There were just too many people in it to concentrate solely on her."

The series, in fact, would rely not only on a huge and somewhat rotating ensemble, but on characters dead or soon to die. In the beginning there would be two East Texas oil wildcatters, Digger Barnes and Jock Ewing— partners, for a time. But Jock would burn Digger on an oil deal, pocketing the lion's share of the profits and then turning his attention to Digger's longtime love, Miss Ellie Southworth. Miss Ellie—in her day, a Scarlett O'Hara understudy if there ever was one—would in the meantime be looking for a miracle by which to save her family's all-important Southfork Ranch from bankruptcy.

And so it would unfold: Jock would save Miss Ellie's ranch, Miss Ellie would marry Jock, and Digger would be left face down in a trough of rotgut. The Ewing couple would give birth to three boys: John Ross, Gary and Bobby. Gary, an alcoholic ne'er-do-well, would be tossed out early in the series (and reappear in "Knots Landing"), leaving behind his libidinous daughter, Lucy. John Ross, the eldest, would seize control of Ewing Oil.

Bobby, it seemed at the outset, would be the crucial Ewing in the series. Once a good-time Charlie, the youngest Ewing would abandon his playboy ways and fall in love with Digger Barnes' alluring daughter, Pamela. The show, then, originally called for the action revolving around the precarious marriage of Bobby and Pamela, trapped between feuding families and surrounded by the temptations garish wealth can bring.

For these critical roles, CBS enlisted the services of Victoria Principal and Patrick Duffy. Duffy, formerly a star in "The Man from Atlantis," was only too happy to shed his webbed feet, but had his objections to a few of the initial scripts. In particular, Duffy wanted to see the playboy image de-emphasized. That was fine with CBS, but the subsequent problem emerged: who would provide the show with the conflict?

The writers did what they could to tighten the screws. Pamela would move in with Bobby, into the veritable belly of the beast, Southfork Ranch. The son of Digger Barnes, Cliff, would swear to avenge his father by driving Ewing Oil out of business. And Miss Ellie would continue to be married to Jock Ewing, but the mere mention of Digger Barnes would reduce her to dreamy-eyed paralysis.

Last but not least, the barbarian acts of the series would be perpetrated in Texas' most sophisticated city. The show, in fact, would be called "Dallas."

Larry Hagman put the pilot script for "The Waverly Wonders" aside and studied the sketch for "Dallas." He then passed it on to Maj. She read it and told her husband, "This is *it*."

Larry agreed. His first impression had been one of wicked delight: "There wasn't one redeeming person in it. Even the mother was bad! I was tired of shows in which everybody was so nice and warm and cuddly. I wanted to see some ass kickers."

Still, it seemed obvious to him that the writers didn't have a good grasp of the *real* Texas. But, he said, "I figured to fix that. I knew about these people—they were friends of Pappy's. Larger than life. They money you to death, use it like a club to make people do what they want. Women are chattel to be bought or sold. The ladies understand that and act accordingly. The object is to marry the rich one, have a couple of kids, get in that little ol' divorce court and sue for everything you can get. . . .

"I knew if they gave me my head, I could make it live."

But Larry's suspicions, borne out of previous failures, resurfaced upon talking with Lorimar Productions. No, they told Hagman, J.R. Ewing would not be *the* star—it would be an ensemble cast of *eight* main characters. And as a result, no, the pay would not be commensurate with top-billing fee.

Three times Lorimar made Hagman offers. Three times he refused them. Then came a final offer and the hook: famed stage actress Barbara Bel Geddes would play J.R.'s mother, Miss Ellie, in the series.

"When they told me Barbara was playing my mother," he later recounted, "I said now you're talkin'—if you're going first class, I won't worry about the money. She's a true actress, can't do anything phony, and it makes the show. I can chew up the scenery, as long as she keeps the reality there."

The final offer Larry would term "insulting, but I can live with it." In truth, for all of his haggling with Lorimar, Larry badly wanted the part of J.R. Ewing, enough to read for it. It wasn't just that the role was a leading one, or that he would be flanked by Barbara Bel Geddes. It wasn't even that finally—after playing Barbara Eden's workhorse, Henry Fonda's humble servant, Raquel Welch's buffoon and prime-time television's straight guy—he would finally get a character which could steal a show.

No, the real drive to portray J.R. stemmed from those tepid summer mornings in Weatherford, when a teenage boy would awaken to find a jeep parked on his parents' front porch, then would follow his father to the courthouse and hear the rough-hewn talk of thieves and braggarts. Lost in a Hemingway novel in Vermont, the boy would dream his way back to Possum Canyon Lake or the Gulf Coast, imagining himself by his father's side, wrestling with a largemouth bass at the end of a bamboo cane pole. The boy would grow up and move to Europe, then to New York and finally to Malibu Beach . . . but there would still be a boy's awe in the man's heart, and an elephant's memory of Benjamin Jackson Hagman in his eldest son's fondest thoughts.

"My dad knew about stuff like this," Hagman would say of the show's malicious characters. "Of course, he was not as ruthless as J.R.

"But in a way," he added, "I get to play *him*."

* * *

On one level, it seemed the worst of times to introduce a soap opera to the prime-time audience. The formula had been taken as far as it could go, many said; it couldn't possibly go any further without incurring disastrous ratings. In fact, the evening precursors to "Dallas" were soap spoofs like "Soap" and "Mary Hartman, Mary Hartman," which scored points by lampooning rather than glorifying the soap-opera tradition. Presumably, these two shows constituted the last word on soaps.

Yet according to Jack Craine, CBS' director of television programming, "Suddenly advertisers woke up to the fact that the afternoon serials aimed at women weren't finding an audience. Many of those women were now working out in the daytime." Could it then not be, wondered the producers, that women who weren't getting their soap fix in the afternoon might be susceptible in the evening? And, assuming the heightened production values of the seventies sped up the action and used sharper camera work, couldn't men and teenagers be drawn into the drama as well?

"Dallas," like all soap operas, would rely on what could be termed the Scheherezade Principle: "Leave 'em wanting more." It was a tried-and-true principle, but prime-time sponsors continually balked at the notion, arguing that it would be impossible for a viewer to comprehend the third show if he had not seen the previous two episodes. As a result, "Dallas" scriptwriters worked on self-contained plots for the telling first five episodes of the series, until it became apparent that with so many characters and subplots, the show required a sprawling, dangling, forever unresolved approach.

But initially, the producers had to act with caution. As Jim Davis, who would play Jock Ewing, observed, "We came down here to make a five-part miniseries with no idea of what would happen to it after that. We didn't know whether it would go or not."

And it almost didn't. The first five episodes of "Dallas," in retrospect, were among the series' most cumbersome, replete with wooden dialogue and—as will be detailed in the next chapter—preposterous Hollywood visions of what Texas must be like. Bobby and Pamela were *too* nice; Jock and Miss Ellie recited their Texanisms without a shred of Southern soul; and the scriptwriters, in their effort to provide self-contained story lines, throttled the last vestiges of realism.

J.R. Ewing's wife, played by Linda Gray, did not even have a name during those first five episodes; in those shows, Sue Ellen was "honey" and "darlin'" and had a grand total of four lines. The J.R. character was also underdeveloped. Originally, Hagman, like Duffy, had also complained about his character's demeanor, but in the opposite way: he thought J.R. wasn't *bad* enough.

The writers complied to some degree, but in wrestling with the issue of J.R.'s meanness, the question surfaced: how far can you take a villain during family hour? Traditionally, a prime-time show—be it sitcom or drama—would feature antagonists, but seldom, if ever, would they triumph over the starring protagonist, who would embody various compellingly American traits. Could the audience swallow the notion of J.R. sticking it to Bobby? How would they react if the bad guy always prevailed?

In this, more than any other area, "Dallas" had no prime-time precedent to follow.

But Larry Hagman followed his instincts, and in so doing J.R. Ewing became the crown prince—albeit black prince—of prime-time.

"Seeing people lying and cheating! Avarice! Sex! Greed! That's what people like," Larry Hagman would enthuse. "Texans use money like clubs. They don't brook no deterrent in their spiraling upwards. Anything that interferes is in danger of extinction."

What people wanted to see, in Larry's view, was what he saw in Weatherford. He called Texas "air-conditioned street theater" and called Texans "the Greeks of America." This was the kind of outrageousness, he said, that audiences would clamor to see.

"As a Texan, I've always found myself a little outside the realm of reality," he said. "I think Texans are special people. A little crazy, maybe, but I believe we are different from other Americans in some ways. There's a myth that sets Texans apart from other people, and they believe it. It's a country where you drive 400 miles for a dinner date. The climate and the soil are brutal. You have to be tough to survive. But Texas is beautiful, too."

What Larry Hagman had in mind for J.R. Ewing was a metaphor of the Lone Star State: wicked but irresistable, crude but enigmatic. Inevitably, he acknowledged, the show would overplay the Texas frontier schtick. (His friends told him the first episodes of "Dallas" were "the best science-fiction thing they ever saw." He explained to them that efforts to convince the producers that real Dallasites don't wear bandanas and cowboy hats failed.) But in J.R. Ewing, Larry Hagman would stake his claim to the truth.

"I have elicited this character from real life," he would tell several reporters. "There's no kidding about it. . . . I know so many Texans who are the epitome of this dude. People get wealthy, and they get mean."

But when Larry recalled the "mean dudes" he met or

heard tell about in Texas, he thought of bigamists, anarchists and husband-killers. Prime-time wouldn't go for such high dosages of brutal reality. Another approach would have to be taken.

The solution resided in Larry Hagman, actor. In the absence of J.R. Ewing, "Dallas" was and is a well-produced soap opera; with J.R., it's hyperbole, and thus borderline comedy. Packaging evil on evening television, as Hagman would demonstrate, could be accomplished only by combining realism with a sort of campy sensibility.

In J.R.'s case, it's the boyish malevolence of his sudden smile, the feigned politeness and mock surprise, the backslapping and grouchy impatience that make him unmistakeably creepy—evil, in fact, in the fine tradition of Boris Karloff monster movies. And yet Larry Hagman's character, however evil, is a monster about whom no human could ever suffer a nightmare.

Better still, Larry's J.R. actually represented an *enviable* evil. As the introduction to this book details, those without a sense of humor could actually make the case that "Dallas," through J.R., effectively *sells* evil. Who could help but grudgingly admire a man who hoards women, punishes his foes and laughs all the way to the bank?

Hagman himself said in the early days of "Dallas," "I hope I'm typecast like this the rest of my life. I'll tell you honestly, playing this part is like falling off a log. Now Bobby, he's got the hardest job of all. He's got to be nice all the time—honey this and dear that. One of these days he's going to go berserk and chop everybody up. But I get to play out my fantasies. I get the girls. I get to stab everybody in the back."

In the wake of goodie two-shoes shows like "Little House on the Prairie," the J.R. character blew in like a coastal breeze on a Texas summer afternoon. Enthused one critic, "Larry Hagman as J.R. Ewing is a most satisfying villain, especially in an era when heroes, anointed with the blessings of ambivalence, have all the good lines and evil is commonly represented by inarticulate psychopaths; Hagman's J.R. has a touch of Tennessee Williams's mean, weak young Southern gentlemen, a touch of old, snarly Dan Duryea, and a good deal of his own soft, spacy charm."

A number of critics have commented on the biblical underpinnings of "Dallas." Script after script recalls Cain and Abel, Abraham and Isaac, Noah and his sons and Sodom and Gomorrah. And throughout each slithered J.R. Ewing, a snake with venom masking itself as charm. Despite his mother's proclamation of "Why J.R., you don't have a redeeming bone in your body," the eldest Ewing son didn't attain his position of power strictly by bludgeoning everyone in his path. Like that master of politicians, Lyndon Johnson, J.R. knew when to squeeze a shoulder and woo a power broker. Like Johnson, J.R. had the ability to wrap his threats in velvet and belittle a pretender through a sweet white smile.

And with Hagman's tall, solid frame and dignified military strut, J.R. Ewing had the look of a "man's man," the type women can't stay away from and other men find themselves grudgingly admiring. Nothing sissified about J.R.'s good looks: just blue eyes that could register sincerity or vindictiveness, a conservative but full haircut, and a square jaw embellished by just enough flesh to add a vaguely youthful touch.

Finally, J.R. Ewing possessed a subliminal power in the eyes of the audience, a touch that only Larry Hagman could provide: this heartless, adulterous cad had once been a sweet, eager-to-please astronaut! The perversion of "I Dream of Jeannie"'s Major Anthony Nelson was one of those added strokes of genius for which no human could be responsible. But there it was, even if the audience wasn't fully aware of its manifestations.

But not all of what went into shaping J.R. involved mere instinct and good fortune. Much of it took hard work for Larry—the same kind of effort he had expended in the modest successes of his past. Recalling his days in "The Edge of Night," Larry applied his same methods of preparation to "Dallas": picking out the hard scenes, learning and relearning them, then dictating his share of the dialogue into a tape recorder along with various ideas regarding inflection and body movement. Replaying the tape, he would then alter the dialogue slightly, tossing out extraneous words and adding a Southern texture to the phrasing.

The whole cast wanted "Dallas" to be a success, of course. But it was Larry who wanted to make the show *true*. J.R. was his gesture to Ben Hagman and the other giants of his youth, as well as the culmination of all his experience as an actor. This one would count. He would see to that.

The redoubtable J. R. Ewing, at peace with himself. (RDR Productions)

Mary Martin and her nineteen-year-old son Larry crooning "Get Out Those Old Records" in 1950. As evidenced by this early photograph, the two seemed more like sister and brother than mother and son. The former Peter Pan and the present J. R. Ewing weren't always close, but today Mary and Larry enjoy a marvelous relationship. (Neal Peters Collection)

Twenty-three-year-old Larry Hagman and his fiancée, Swedish-born Maj Irene Axelsson. They met while Larry was a sergeant in the Air Force in 1954; over thirty years later, Larry and Maj continue to be happily married. (AP/Wide World Photos)

Larry's undistinguished stage career ended in 1962 with The Beauty Part, *starring Bert Lahr. The Broadway play flopped, having opened during New York's sixteen-week newspaper strike. (Dan Yakir/Phototeque)*

Jeannie (Barbara Eden) and Major Anthony Nelson (Hagman) in "I Dream of Jeannie," the television sitcom that put Larry's career in high gear. (Frank Edwards/Fotos International)

Barbara Eden and Larry Hagman at an NBC affiliates party in 1966. Larry's success due to "I Dream of Jeannie" became a mixed blessing as celebrity pressures mounted and forced him into forty thousand dollars worth of psychotherapy sessions. (Frank Edwards/Fotos International)

Larry's first motion picture, Fail Safe in 1964. As the Russian interpreter for the president (Henry Fonda), Larry's role was a plum and led to other acting bids—though never to fame on the silver screen. (Dan Yakir/ Phototeque)

Brooding in The Cavern *in 1965.* (Dan Yakir/Phototeque)

With Joanna Pettet in The Group *in 1966. As with "I Dream of Jeannie," The Group saw heavy interaction between Larry and females—but no sex. That came later in "Dallas."* (Dan Yakir/Phototeque)

With wife, Maj, at the Hollywood premiere of Head, *1968.* (Frank Edwards/Fotos International)

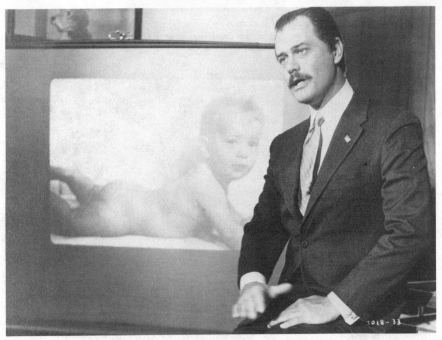

Looking like Jack Nicholson in 3 in the Cellar, *1970.* (Dan Yakir/Phototeque)

One of Larry's better movie roles was as an oversexed ambulance driver in Mother, Jugs & Speed *in 1976.* (Dan Yakir/Phototeque)

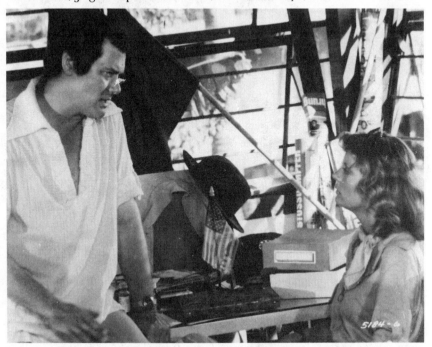

As a race promoter with Susan Sarandon in Checkered Flag or Crash, *1977.* (Dan Yakir/Phototeque)

Almost unrecognizable as a colonel in The Eagle Has Landed, *which also starred Michael Caine, Donald Sutherland, and Robert Duvall. (Dan Yakir/Phototeque)*

One big happy family: the Ewings of "Dallas" rack up a People's Choice award in 1980 for Best TV Show. From left to right: (front) Charlene Tilton (Lucy Ewing), Barbara Bel Geddes (Miss Ellie Ewing), Linda Gray (Sue Ellen Ewing); (back) Patrick Duffy (Bobby Ewing), Jim Davis (Jock Ewing), Larry Hagman (J. R. Ewing), Steve Kanaly (Ray Krebbs, Jock's son through a previous marriage). (Frank Edwards/Fotos International)

America's favorite couple, J. R. and Sue Ellen—shown here as Larry and Linda. (Scott Downie/Celebrity Photo)

Ever the practical man, Larry sometimes wears this solar air-conditioned pith helmet when the Dallas temperatures soar at Southfork. (Akhtar Hussein/SIPA/ Special Features)

At night in New York, on the other hand, Larry prefers the more noticeable attire. (RPM/ SIPA/Special Features)

With close friend Carroll O'Connor, TV's memorable Archie Bunker on "All in the Family," in 1979. The cigar in O'Connor's hand is permanent; the fat on Larry's cheeks was not, as a fasting program in 1980 allowed him to shed over forty pounds. (Frank Edwards/Fotos International)

Handing out phony $100 bills at London's Heathrow Airport in 1980 while the world waited to find out who shot J. R. (Syndication International/Photo Trends)

While the rest of the "Dallas" cast stewed in record Dallas temperatures, Larry pranced through the Royal Ascot, upstaging the queen and gaining fine publicity as his agents wrangled with Lorimar Productions and CBS over a new contract for Larry. (Syndication International/Photo Trends)

Bobby and J. R. Ewing. While Larry expressed sadness over Patrick Duffy's decision to leave "Dallas," other cast members felt that Duffy had cut off his nose to spite his face. (Dan Yakir/Phototeque)

On the day "Dallas" killed off Bobby Ewing, the heartless J. R. could be found playing alongside renowned flutist James Galway, under the direction of Dallas Symphony Orchestra conductor Eduardo Mata. (Jason Fraser/SIPA/Special Features)

Larry with his favorite device, a battery-operated fan that blows cigarette smoke back into the offending party's face. Behind Larry is a painting by his daughter, Heidi. (Ron Galella)

Larry with mother, Mary, upon receiving his gold star on the famous Hollywood Walk of Fame. (Ron Wolfson/RETNA Ltd.)

With Maj at a masquerade ball for charity in Los Angeles. *(Steve Granitz/Celebrity Photo)*

The Hagmans, Thanksgiving 1982 in New York: Heidi, Larry, Maj, and Preston. *(Ron Galella)*

Larry in his "Malibu Mission" bedroom. (Richard Fish/Shooting Star)

Maj Hagman, a model of toleration, with her Texas chieftan. (Richard Fish/Shooting Star)

A legend in his own time. (Ron Galella)

CHAPTER SEVEN

Dateline: Dallas

Some Texans say I don't know what I'm talking about. But I know about the oil interests. I worked for an oil tool factory and I've seen what those big shots do to one another. If we told the real story, they'd blow up CBS.

—Larry Hagman

As with all subsequent episodes, the "Dallas" miniseries began with sweeping aerial views of the nation's eighth largest city. With the show's theme song (a stirring nod to Prokofiev's *Romeo and Juliet*) galloping in the background, cut after cut revealed slices of Dallas: the relentless Central Expressway traffic; the gleaming corporate spires of the Central Business District; the Cotton Bowl, home of the Dallas Cowboys football team. And yes, a few scenes depicted the rural outlying areas, complete with cattle and farm implements. That seemed fair enough, since much of Texas remains rooted in agriculture and livestock. For the most part, the opening cuts of "Dallas" portrayed the city as it is: sprawling, sophisticated, ambitious and fast-paced.

But as the five shows unfolded, a troubling pattern began to emerge. The "Dallas" premiere revealed palm trees rooted firmly in the middle of downtown Dallas. From the window of J.R.'s office on One Main Place, a curtain of blue ocean was plainly visible. Later in the show, a hurricane struck the city.

Beautiful images, each of them. However, as a number of Texas journalists were gracious enough to point out in print, hurricanes, by their very nature, have never hit Dallas or any other Texas city that is not on the Gulf Coast. Dallas, they explained, was not only nowhere near the Gulf Coast, but in truth was the nation's largest landlocked city—a fact that would also raise questions about J.R.'s ocean view. And the only thing even close to resembling palm trees in the city's business district were the upright parking meters.

And so it went. Scene after scene fortified the creeping suspicion that despite the presence of Larry Hagman, "Dallas" knew nothing about Dallas. Producer Leonard Katzman seemed nonplussed. "We couldn't figure out what to call it, a hurricane or a tornado—we just needed a lot of wind," he explained. Pressed to identify the source of the TV show's knowledge about Dallas, Katzman admitted that the first five episodes were written not on the basis of consultation with Texas experts, but rather with the help of an L.A. research service. And, he added, the remaining thirteen shows in the first season of "Dallas" would continue to rely on information from the West Coast.

Local critics took aim and fired. One TV reporter dismissed the show as "video trash." Another wrote, "It would be simpleminded to expect fidelity to fact from fantasy. And yet the persistence of certain stereotypes is an irritant like a blister on a heel."

How did the Ewings manage to coast from one place to another without having to endure the traffic jams of the Central Expressway? Where did all the downtown parking spaces come from? Why did all the women sit by the pool in evening dresses?

But most of all, what was the deal with all the boots and cowboy hats? Why were the producers pretending that Dallas is a city of oil and cattle? And as for the dialogue:

"Mama don't allow no business talk with supper on the table."

"You and me, honey—it was good, real good. You and me shoulda been hitched a long time ago."

Did *anyone* in Dallas talk like that anymore? Did *anyone* in the city *ever* wear bandanas and ride horses? Could the creators of "Dallas" have been any further off base?

Larry had told the media that he had passed on the initial "Dallas" scripts to Mary Martin, who supposedly had commented, "Why, this sounds just like Weatherford!" At the same time, the glaring incongruities didn't escape Larry's notice. But, he promised, "I aim to fix that."

It would be an uphill battle. For starters, none of the scriptwriters, including creator David Jacobs, had ever visited Dallas. Jacobs, in fact, had been quite candid about his ignorance: "I don't know Texas. I was just working off the connotations, and Dallas sounded like pure Texas. I wrote the first draft off the top of my head. I was writing for the image and not really about the place. After all, there are J.R.s on Wall Street, there are J.R.s in New England textile mills. God knows there are J.R.s in the movie business in L.A."

No one could argue with that contention. But where

69

Jacobs missed the boat was in his notion that "Dallas sounded like pure Texas."

The Lone Star State's second-largest city is, in fact, its *least* Southern area. "I think a lot of people within Dallas consider Dallas *not* to be in Texas," says Ruth Fitzgibbons Miller, editor of the city magazine *D*. "We think of ourselves instead as a can-do place, a city of the future. The city's pretty far removed from its stereotype."

The stereotype portrayed in "Dallas," actually, seemed more reminiscent of another Texas city—Dallas' metroplex sister, Fort Worth, a cosmopolitan cowtown if there ever was one. Even Houston, with its oil-based economy and bevy of country-western nightclubs, might have fit the bill.

It's true, of course, that Dallas is a city that cares deeply about money. When John Neely Bryan pitched tent in the flat meadowlands of North Texas in the early nineteenth century, he proclaimed the area an ideal center for trade. Since then, Dallas has indeed been big on commerce—whether one looks at the city's tremendous banking business (tops in the state), its unsurpassed Market Center or its appetite for lavish stores like Neiman-Marcus. But the Dallas economy relies less on "Texas tea" and more on insurance, real estate, high technology and defense contracts. (In fact, to date, no oil has ever been struck in Dallas County—or even in Collin County, the location of the Ewings' Southfork Ranch.) When the Dallas chamber of commerce pushes its city, it talks about Dallas/Fort Worth Airport (the nation's largest), the futuristic downtown skyline and the economic growth outstripping that of almost every city in the nation.

Publicity-wise, Dallas had always kept a low profile until 1963, when Lee Harvey Oswald foreclosed that possibility. Smaller than Houston, less naturally abundant than Austin and San Antonio, and far less cosmopolitan or historical than the nation's other big cities, Dallas now had one more rap against it: the world would remember it as the city where President John F. Kennedy was shot. It seemed that Dallas would have no choice but to forget the past, shed all stereotypes and live for the future.

Yet Dallas continued to be a self-conscious city, envious of the glamour of California and New York and determined to keep up with (and maybe one day surpass) the coastal Joneses. Rediscovering its urban core, the city's movers and shakers pumped millions into the central business district, not stopping until their downtown had become the nation's most modern. Millions more were allocated for new museums and a state-of-the-art symphony hall. Even Dallas' football team, the Cowboys, announced that it was "America's Team"—to which then-Houston Oilers coach Bum Phillips replied, "Yeah, but we're Texas' team."

Which suited Dallas just fine: the city had big plans and a brand new image in the works. And now along came "Dallas" with its California scriptwriters and its actors clumsily aping Texana. Worst of all, along came native son Larry Hagman, a man who claimed to know the region inside out, but whose character embodied all that was foul and deceitful about the wrongheaded stereotype! The outside world would be brutally misled!

"Dallas is street theater," Hagman said. "You don't have to make it up." He was referring to H.L. Hunt and T. Cullen Davis, each having once been embroiled in scandals bespeaking of wealth's grotesqueries. And, of course, he was thinking of his father's friends in the forties and fifties. But this was 1978. While Larry was away, Dallas had discarded its spurs.

For a long time, then, Dallas refused to embrace "Dallas." Many simply ignored the show, while others watched the plots stumble along with snide amusement. But others found nothing to laugh about in "Dallas." An oil executive expressed his disgust toward J.R. Ewing and concluded, "We can only hope the show will go away soon."

A local congressman remarked that the show's glamorous depiction of Dallas had made it difficult for him to convince his fellow congressmen that some Texans are poor and out of work. At the same time, he said, "Dallas" portrayed Dallas as a twisted autocracy: "The idea that one family could play such a big role in the city today is ridiculous."

Hagman had publicly asserted, tongue in cheek, that Dallas women "are chattel" and that they understand this "and act accordingly." Certainly the series believed this, dealing as it did with jewelry-bedecked money chasers and placing nearly every woman in the cast squarely under J.R.'s heel. But female community leaders in real life wondered aloud: Why don't these "Dallas" women have jobs? Why do they always dress like high-priced call girls? And what in the world do they see in a mysogenic troll like J.R. Ewing?

Of course, several aspects of "Dallas" had basis in fact. Dallas *does* have a Petroleum Club and an Oil Barons' Ball. Southfork Ranch *does* exist, a few miles outside the city limits. The city *does* have an inordinate number of Mercedes Benzes cluttering its freeways. And despite its political conservatism, Dallas *does* breed or attract marital strife (in fact, it boasts the nation's highest divorce rate).

Dallas even has a Ewing Avenue, a Ewing Oil Company, and an unfortunate soul named J.R. Ewing living just outside the city limits. (Mr. Ewing regularly received nuisance calls from all over the world until he removed his phone number from the listings.) But what the city doesn't have are businessmen who dress like J.R. All of a sudden, the Dallas chamber of commerce found itself having to apologize to chagrined visitors for not providing a city adorned in Stetsons and kicker boots.

Some of the cast members made earnest attempts to emulate reality. Linda Gray developed a subtle drawl and logged several hours at Neiman-Marcus, observing how the customers dressed and wore their hair. Jim Davis and Barbara Bel Geddes made slight adjustments to their vocal cadences, but mainly concentrated on the slow, expansive gestures and gazes of weathered Southerners.

Others, like Victoria Principal and Ken Kercheval, demonstrated less success at conveying the Texas within their characters. This might have been fitting for first-generation Dallasites, but not for the offspring of Digger Barnes. Yet the locals seemed more annoyed at the bogus Texification of the dialogue than at the inflection. Wrote *Dallas Times-Herald* TV critic Dick Hitt:

> *There seem to be more and more viewers each week losing touch with "Dallas," the television miniseries about big money, dark intrigue and brooding genes that takes place right chere in our little ol' town. That is the way they're havin' us all talk, doncha know, as they depict whut lafe is lak in Big D. By losing touch, I refer to the growing numbers of locals who have stopped asking each other each Monday if they watched it the night before and who are saying "No," or "Hell, no," or "Lan' sakes, yew must be tetched in the haid if you thank ah'm still watchin' 'at piece a junk."*

Like other critics, however, Hitt went out of his way to exempt Larry Hagman from the castigation, saying that the actor "has done a good job of recalling what a Weatherford accent sounds like. The lines of dialogue he has been given aren't his fault . . ."

Larry, in fact, had been caught dead in the middle of

the authenticity conflict. As one of the show's stars, he willingly trumpeted the virtues of "Dallas," seldom failing to add that the show was as realistic as television audiences could bear. On the other hand, Larry knew better, and doing it right was something he didn't take lightly.

Juanita Hagman remembers Larry visiting Weatherford during the early days of "Dallas," and taking great pains to jot down anything anyone said that had an unmistakeable Texas ring to it. Within a short period of time, his own Texas accent returned, as did a few memories of Texas life that he relayed to the scriptwriters and producers. Some were vetoed, like Larry's recollection of a Weatherford millionaire's funeral, during which the high-school band played (although the only tune it knew was the school fight song) and the millionaire's favorite palomino and dog were killed and buried alongside him.

But those areas pertaining to the J.R. character were Larry's singular domain. Cowboy hat and boots notwithstanding, his portrayal of a ruthless Texas businessman was all too real. Had someone with a weaker grasp on regional mannerisms played J.R., doubtless few oilmen would have bothered to complain about the image they were being tagged with. Their objection, in fact, was that Hagman's J.R. was *thoroughly* believable. The reptilian eyes, the shameless swagger, the bottomless insincerity of his smile and the manipulative "Southern manners"—it was all there.

Even off-camera, Larry had seemingly transformed himself into the "Dallas" viper. Journalists spread the word that sure, Hagman was a devoted family man, but he didn't hang up his cruel smile at the studio before going home. Recalling a scene where J.R., while still in bed with his sister-in-law Kristin, makes a phone call to ensure that her boyfriend will never work in the South again as an attorney, an interviewer wondered aloud whether or not anyone would ever do such a thing.

"Shitfire," replied Hagman. "I've seen it happen in this town. I've even done it myself."

Larry had "become" J.R., and so in turn did "Dallas." Responding to popular and critical demand, the script-writers began to de-emphasize Bobby and Pamela, there-after turning their attention to the other Ewing couple. Having been neglected in the previous five scripts, Sue Ellen and John Ross Ewing were literally fleshed out be-fore the audience's eyes. This spontaneous approach achieved remarkable results. Far less contrived than the other "Dallas" characters, J.R. and Sue Ellen could thrust and parry within the context of the daily drama rather than being shackled from the get-go by an outsider's di-mensionless character sketch.

Before long, J.R. had become *the* pivotal character of "Dallas." Said one scriptwriter, "I mean, who's going to believe this stuff without Larry to make it work? He is also the best actor. No matter how far out the script, he never fools around with the reality of the character."

Gradually, it began to matter less and less how one felt about some of the other characters or some of the di-alogue, or even some of the plots. What mattered was whether or not you liked watching J.R. do his dastardly thing. If you loved to hate J.R., it turned out, you would probably find yourself among the "Dallas" faithful.

And that became the tag of Larry's J.R.: "the man ev-eryone loves to hate." It sounded so simple that people tended to forget the rarity of Hagman's feat. How often does an audience "love to hate" a character? Instances crop up in plays (Cyril Ritchard's Captain Hook in *Peter Pan*) and in movies (Louise Fletcher's Nurse Ratchett in *One Flew Over the Cuckoo's Nest*). But in a television series,

75

the recurrence of a villain has usually meant the bad guy must be either completely hapless or completely loathsome. J.R. Ewing was neither, for J.R. was *real*. He could be your employer or your husband or your brother—a creep, but "sometimes he's really not such a bad guy."

You couldn't trust J.R. Ewing, but you could *believe* him. And within him resided a sense of place, but he also transcended that. J.R. could be anywhere.

But, as it turned out, J.R. was in Dallas. By the end of the second season, Robert Folsom—the city's mayor at the time—decided to bury any ill feelings between Dallas and "Dallas." Mayor Folsom and his entourage drove to the Southfork ranch, met the cast and officially declared it "'Dallas' Day." Folsom and Hagman traded good-natured gibes over barbeque and then the mayor left, singing the show's praises although remarking that "I don't recognize any of the characters" in the city's real life.

Soon, Dallas became the second home for "Dallas" employees during the city's blazing summers. Coping with the chiggers in the Southfork grass had been trying enough, but at times some of the cast members nearly wilted under the heat. Eventually, the producers began to keep their stars inside until the last possible moment, and equip them with bibs so that the makeup wouldn't run off their sweaty faces and onto their wardrobes. In the face of such discomfort, Larry Hagman would stroll around carefree, a solar-cooled pith helmet perched on top of his head.

Inevitably, the "Dallas" characters began to venture outside of Southfork and into the city itself. At the height of the show's popularity in 1980, Victoria Principal was horrified to discover that all traffic on a Dallas freeway had stopped—because the drivers surrounding her car had recognized her. Larry was seen at various local haunts, sipping on Ramos Gin Fizzes and communing with the natives. He especially liked a video bar called On the Air, where he once looked up at the video screen and was surprised to see Major Anthony Nelson cavorting with Jeannie.

Sometimes the fascination had its limits. One bartender groused to the papers about Charlene Tilton incessantly ordering her "special margarita." Critics continued to take a few scattered jabs, giggling about singer Barry Gibb's very public depression over being dumped by Principal and occasionally announcing that "the 'Dallas' fad is over."

For the most part, however, the city delighted in having stars like Hagman peopling their bars. Furthermore, "Dallas" had begun to have favorable economic impact on the city—a sure-fire way to please the community leaders. Being a "right-to-work" (i.e. no mandatory unions) state, Texas had always been a cheap location site for movies. Soon, "Dallas" began to take advantage of this situation as well, hiring scores of local studio technicians and hundreds of extras for the show's location scenes. Amateurs would travel from all over the state just to earn thirty-five dollars daily and be able to say to their friends that "I got to be an actor on 'Dallas.'"

And as a shrewd publicity gesture toward the city, on one occasion the city's leading socialites were formally invited by the "Dallas" producers to participate in a scene that, in fact, involved a party of Dallas bigwigs. The real-life bigwigs turned out in droves, and the scene scored well, although viewers would never be able to tell that the extras were the genuine article. ("It's like wearing silk underwear," explained Linda Gray. "No one needs to know but you.")

By 1980, tourism in Dallas had increased remarkably. Many of the visitors were from out of the country, and the first question they would ask was, "Where's J.R.?"

The results of this curiosity were not merely economic. By 1985, surveys showed that the foremost tourist attraction in Dallas, by far, was no longer Dealy Plaza—the site of JFK's assassination—but rather Southfork Ranch. In fact, Dealy wasn't even second, having fallen behind Neiman-Marcus (which was milking "Dallas" fashions for all they were worth).

Few failed to comprehend the implications of this. The Kennedy assassination—for so many years the millstone around Dallas' neck—had finally been erased from public consciousness. Its replacement was . . . well, perhaps a myth. But it was a myth with some roots in truth, a myth people had fun with, and a myth that made money.

How much? In 1985 alone, it was estimated that between tourism, revenues generated from the Southfork property and fees for services rendered by extras and other local help, "Dallas" pumped $30 million into the Dallas economy.

By the early eighties, the city began to acknowledge its gratitude in full force. Leonard Katzman received the Dallas Communications Council's Communicator of the Year Award in 1984, was made an honorary citizen and received a proclamation from then Governor Mark White. A year later, White appeared on camera to commemorate the show's 200th episode, and was filmed waving to a nonexistent rodeo crowd.

By that time, most of the local T.V. critics had warmed to "Dallas." Partly this was because the show provided a ready source of material; for many, however, it was simply a matter of acceptance. After all, wrote one reporter, "Can you imagine a true-to-life series based on the *real* Dallas, the real people like you and me? How about the saga of a North Dallas insurance agent going home on the Central Expressway to grill Safeway rib-eyes on his backyard hibachi?"

Indeed, it came to pass that many Dallasites enjoyed

the "Dallas" myth far more than the Dallas reality. The show, wrote one journalist, "sustains an illusion about the rough charm of this prairie metropolis, which some natives prefer to the bland, buttoned-down business efficiency closer to the heart of the Dallas of the 1970s."

By degrees, some noticed, fantasy and reality had actually converged. Chamber of commerce brochures on Dallas, Fort Worth and Arlington all name-dropped J.R. Ewing. Today, a Dallas chamber of commerce vice president proclaims that "There *are* a lot of wheeler-dealers in this city," and throughout Texas self-proclaimed celebrities appear, calling themselves J.R. Knowing that eyes are on them, noted a Dallas journalist, oil executives and socialites were aping certains characteristics of their respective TV characters. "Dallas," concluded the writer, had never been Dallas . . . but Dallas, he said, was fast becoming "Dallas."

"In a way, I think people here are grateful to us," said Linda Gray of her second home. "Because as the show's popularity has grown around the world, it's made them feel important. In a way, the show has made celebrities out of everyone who lives here."

But as Katzman would tell the media, "We're basically interested in the story of the people. It could have been about New Hampshire." What made "Dallas" about Dallas, in spite of the ineptitude of the scriptwriting, was the emergence of J.R. Ewing, guided flawlessly by Larry Hagman.

"I know the guys like the Ewings and they hate me because I'm really onto them," he would laugh. But they would *love* to hate him. In his own way, Hagman would immortalize his mentors.

The world would love J.R. Ewing for his evil ways, and in no better way would they demonstrate this love than to applaud the shadowy figure who would shoot him.

CHAPTER EIGHT

The Shot Heard 'Round the World

We remember people because they make a certain impression on our memory cells. Often, we will recall someone based on a single, unforgettable moment in time.

Despite his decades of public service, no one will ever think of Richard Nixon again without thinking of the Watergate years. Babe Ruth will always be remembered in the context of his 714 home runs, even though Hank Aaron broke that record over a decade ago. The name Robert Oppenheimer meant nothing to us until the day the bombs dropped on Hiroshima.

In the entertainment world, it often takes a singular event to deliver a performer to immortality. Judy Garland's dreamy "Somewhere Over the Rainbow" in *The Wizard of Oz* launched her career to the heavens, and from the moment Vivien Leigh uttered her first haughty "Fiddle-dee-dee!" on *Gone With the Wind,* her future was assured. There was no stopping Elvis Presley and the Beatles after their respective appearances on "The Ed

Sullivan Show," nor could anyone slow the momentum of Bruce Springsteen once Jon Landau announced in *Rolling Stone,* "I have seen the future of rock 'n' roll and its name is Springsteen."

In the world of television, we would remember Rob Reiner because Archie Bunker tagged his character "Meathead." We would remember Jim Nabors for Gomer Pyle's "Gawwww-lee!" We would never forget the people who embodied "two wild and crazy guys," "Sock it to me," "To the moon, Alice!", "Gee, Wally," "Heeeeere's Johnny" and "Oh, Lucy!"

And after CBS shot J.R. Ewing on worldwide television, the chances of forgetting Larry Hagman and "Dallas" vanished into thin air.

Throughout most of the 1978 season, "Dallas" could be found in the ratings dog pile—usually fifty-eighth or so. As the producers began to experiment, however, the serial began its climb. "Dallas" was moved from Sunday night to Friday night, which instantly boosted the ratings. The writers scuttled the "self-contained" plot concept and let the tensions between J.R. and the rest of the world spill over into succeeding episodes. J.R. got meaner, plots got riskier and by November of 1979, "Dallas" had nestled into the Nielsen top ten, positioned at number six.

In its premiere season, few national critics failed to consign "Dallas" to the tar pit. By 1979, most had changed their tune. Representative of prevailing sentiments, one critic remarked that "Dallas" was "just plain sleaze," but went on to confess that it was sleaze he couldn't do without. If J.R. was the man they loved to hate, "Dallas" was the show they hated to love—but they did.

Who would J.R. try to shaft this week? In whose bed

would he lay? And in the face of his evil, what new challenges to happiness would the other characters face? Executive producer Philip Capice said, "Viewers love to see rich people more screwed up than they are. It makes them feel superior." Perhaps more to the point, viewers liked to see wealth on parade, but also liked to see wealth ruin wealth—a reminder amidst the glamour that money isn't everything.

But J.R. would always prevail. His brother, his sister-in-law, his archenemy, his concubines—anyone who stepped in his way paid the price. "Not since John Milton gave Satan all the good lines in *Paradise Lost* has a villain so appalled—and fascinated—the world," wrote one reporter.

And as the eldest son of Jock Ewing committed atrocity after atrocity, the question in every viewer's mind had to be: "When's J.R. gonna get his?"

On March 21, 1980, it happened. John Ross Ewing Jr. sat in his office that evening, basking in self-admiration for a lifetime's worth of mischief. In short order, he had driven one business associate to suicide, had driven another to bankruptcy, and was well on his way to driving his brother out of Southfork, his wife into a mental institution and his lover Kristin into jail on a phony prostitution rap. Not bad for a day's work.

Lost in his rush of self-congratulation, J.R. didn't hear the assailant until it was too late. He looked up just in time to see the bullets fly. Both slugs scored, and the head of Ewing Oil fell to the floor, agonizing in death's cradle.

"We were sitting around," recalled Leonard Katzman, "and Phil Capice says, 'Let's have J.R. get his.' We didn't know who shot him. We said the hell with it, let's shoot him and figure out who did it later."

Who shot J.R.? Not even the producers knew at the

time, and yet the question immediately became *the* question of 1980 (a presidential-election year), and arguably the most-asked question since the disturbing Watergate inquiries. (Of this generation, "Who was Deep Throat?" may continue to be the most nagging.) The problem, of course, was that *anyone* on the show had a motive for the attempted murder. Naturally, the camera work betrayed nothing . . . and just as naturally, the episode happened to be the last of the season.

"We've set up the most successful cliff-hanger in the history of television," proclaimed Larry Hagman. And who could deny it? For the next six months, anxiety over whodunnit would swell to unprecedented proportions, leading to a sort of "Dallas"-mania that would change the fortunes of the show, and those connected with it, for good.

Fittingly, the centerpiece of the controversy was Larry's character. Throughout the series, others would be attacked and/or killed—Bobby, Sue Ellen, Jock, Kristin and seemingly scores of others—and yet far less attention would be generated, simply because viewers cared far more deeply about the hateful J.R. than, say, his all-American brother. Who would have thought that the shooting of a prime-time bad guy would create so much hysteria? Still, it could only have been J.R.

But the ploy was a double-edged sword. CBS and Lorimar Productions would reap enormous benefits from the cliff-hanger, but the implicit concession of the episode—that "Dallas" revolved around J.R.—suddenly put Larry Hagman in an extremely powerful position. During the six-month lull between question and answer, the follow-up query for many became: "Will CBS and J.R. shoot each other?"

In television, ratings make the world go 'round. High marks in the Nielsen ratings mean swarms of advertising dollars, which pay for the shows and for the network bosses' swimming pools. Television executives enjoy critical acclaim and Emmy awards, but given a choice between popular appeal and critical plaudits—well, there's no contest.

While making no high-road pretenses, "Dallas" had brought the critics into its camp. That was nice, but nothing compared to the staggering number of the show's regular American following: 40 million, or nearly twenty percent of the entire country. When the show shot J.R., "Dallas" promptly vaulted up to number one in the ratings . . . and stayed there for the entirety of the following season.

"Dallas" had become the big kid on the block. Things tend to fall your way in that situation, and not by coincidence. Not wanting to waste a top-notch show that no one would watch anyway during the "Dallas" time slot, ABC and NBC promptly inserted weak-sister programs and thus enhanced CBS's stronghold. (The NBC show in that time slot was their "News Magazine with David Brinkley," and the ratings were so anemic that humorist Art Buchwald speculated that perhaps Brinkley shot J.R.)

Additionally, CBS' shows flanking the "Dallas" time slot rode up the ratings on that show's coattails, making an entire viewing evening (and being Friday, a very important one) a lost cause for the other networks. By early 1980, ABC—which had enjoyed the number-one network rating for three years—fell to J.R. and CBS.

And lest anyone think that the man most responsible for this revolution wasn't Sir Hagman, numerous individuals took great pains to underscore the truth. "J.R. and Hagman deserve the country's gratitude for lighting up Friday nights with that barracuda smile," gushed *Time* Magazine in its cover story. Hagman, noted the *New York Times,* "has become something of a national cult hero for playing the most wicked, miserable, vile, scheming, conniving, ruthless, amoral, despicable, selfish, vicious, unprincipled wheeler-dealer to come along in eons." Seemingly every magazine and newspaper in the country, and many more overseas, demanded interviews so that they could spread the word about the *real* man behind J.R.

Larry lapped it up. Always a sucker for attention, it delighted him to convey to an interviewer "the real Larry Hagman" and then about-face with a wicked J.R. grin. But the press became more than an amusement for him; it also became his weapon. For Larry wanted a new contract, and he knew that in this struggle, he'd need every weapon he could get.

J.R. had changed Larry's life—mainly for the better, but the pressures began to mount. Maintaining a private life had become a near impossibility. Being recognized in public was one thing, and being mobbed another matter entirely. At first, it amused Larry that J.R. had transformed him into a national sex symbol; that changed, however, when hordes of females would literally envelop him, demanding kisses and other favors.

The money (around $35,000 per episode) was good, but in light of the circumstances, not good enough. Maybe at the outset of "Dallas" there had been eight stars, but by now that had clearly changed . . . and the special stardom reserved for Larry brought responsibilities the other cast members didn't have to face.

Moreover, the residue of Larry's resentment over not seeing a penny from "I Dream of Jeannie" reruns heightened his convictions to seek a new contract. It galled him that a fair number of people were getting rich marketing J.R. T-shirts, bumper stickers and the like, while the contract with Lorimar and CBS fenced him out of the profit picture.

LARRY HAGMAN

"Dallas" was an expensive show, costing some $700,000 per episode. Each principal star reportedly earned in excess of $250,000 annually. Given a choice in the matter, the executives would be unlikely to toss out more money, even to a show as important as "Dallas."

But this was Larry's chance. The whole world was watching him, thinking about him. J.R. had been shot, and the world desperately needed to know who had done it. That was Larry Hagman's leverage.

Just before the March 21 episode, Larry and Maj Hagman boarded an airplane for London. Ostensibly the couple was on vacation, but Larry acknowledged to the press that putting a little distance between the star and the network might give CBS something to think about. Already the executives had been made aware of Hagman's demands—reportedly $100,000 per episode and the rights to merchandise depicting his face—and the flight to London punctuated the actor's earnestness.

England had been hog-wild over J.R. since "Dallas" first hit shore in 1979. The presence of the Hagmans in the United Kingdom brought the British media out in full force, and Larry milked it for all it was worth. Photographers caused a near riot in Heathrow Airport upon the couple's arrival, elbowing and pushing one another aside while Larry passed out phony $100 bills with his autograph and the motto, "In Hagman We Trust."

But CBS wasn't going to take this lying down. Mustering a brilliant counterattack, they leaked to the press this scenario: Suppose that on the way to the hospital, the ambulance containing J.R. were to crash and explode in flames. Suppose, then, that J.R. would be scarred with massive third-degree burns, and that plastic surgery would be required. And suppose that, the surgery completed, the bandages would finally be removed from the face, revealing . . . Robert Culp.

The tables had been turned. All of a sudden, CBS was using the shooting as a means of forcing compliance. They were putting Larry on the stretcher, and leaving his fate up to speculation.

Larry returned to the States in April to begin work on the Blake Edwards movie, *S.O.B.* On May 12, he huddled with his three representatives from the William Morris Agency in Hollywood: Ed Bondy, Ruth Engelhardt and Jack Grossbart. CBS's counteroffensive was the subject of concern. Would the network let J.R. die? Certainly not; the removal of John Ross Ewing Jr. from "Dallas" would completely overturn the complex checks-and-balance system of the Southfork residents. But would the network go with a new J.R.? Was the Robert Culp threat to be taken seriously? Was Larry Hagman expendable?

Larry decided to take the gamble. They're bluffing, he told his agents. He bought each of them white hats—a reminder that they were "the good guys"—and sent them back to the negotiation table with the message: hold firm. Larry also told them that he didn't want any direct part in the haggling—"I don't want to hear any of the threats," he told them.

By the beginning of June, Larry was still working on *S.O.B.* and the negotiations were getting sticky. Thinking that a little more pressure might not hurt, he returned to London on the ninth and continued his waltz with the publicity factory. At the Royal Ascot horse races, Larry appeared in an oh-so-dashing top hat and cane, upstaging Her Majesty in the process. The following day, papers all over the world featured photos of His Nastiness.

In a London radio station, Larry hooked up with an ersatz country-western band and recorded "My Favorite

Sins"—to the tune of "My Favorite Things," but dissimilar in every other way. Crooned J.R. in his smug baritone, "I like to be nasty, I like to be hated, I'd like to be voted the cad of the year." His favorite sins included seeing his business partners bust, cheating at poker, leering at nubiles and messing up the lives of his brothers. Punctuated by evil little chuckles, "My Favorite Sins" gained instant heavy-rotation airplay and galvanized the link between Larry, J.R. and "Dallas."

On June 12, during Texas' most punishing heat wave in recent memory, the cast returned to Dallas to begin shooting. Larry, however, was at Madame Tussaud's wax museum in London, being measured for a statue.

Speculation had it that the other cast members were peeved by Larry's holdout. Publicly, at least, it didn't show. "Sure, we've got a lot of different-type folks on this show," said Jim Davis. "Larry, he's the glue."

On June 17, the agents in the white hats called Larry. CBS and Lorimar were holding firm. Was Larry still committed?

Gut-check time. "We're committed," he told them.

On June 20, the agents again telephoned Larry. They would have an answer by tomorrow. Larry promptly flew to the Bahamas to be closer to the States, and thus the filming location, in the event of good news.

Two days later, Larry Hagman booked a flight back to Dallas. The deal was a sweet one: an estimated $75,000 per episode, plus a share of the merchandising profits. "I'm doing all right," admitted Larry, "but the government takes half, the agent takes 10 percent, the press agent and legal people take huge chunks, and by the time you're through, you've got a living wage."

Maybe so, but Larry Hagman's new "living wage" would make him among the highest-paid series actors in television. J.R. himself would have been proud.

*   *   *

But what *about* J.R.?

"At last count [in 1980]," wrote *Time,* "300 million souls in fifty-seven countries shared this benign obsession. When the Ewing family saga begins its new season, the number is sure to be swollen by millions more who will have succumbed to the summer-long blitz of news features, promotions and gossip. Competing networks are advised to broadcast test patterns."

Whodunit? Was it Sue Ellen, whom J.R. had driven to the bottle and perhaps to incarceration? Cliff Barnes, who had sworn revenge on his archenemy? Dusty Farlow, who had been Sue Ellen's lover and who had supposedly died in a plane crash, but whose body had never been found? Alan Beam the lawyer or Vaughn Leland the banker, two of J.R.'s most recent corporate corpses? Marilee Stone, whose husband had killed himself over a J.R. deal? Kristin Shepard, Sue Ellen's sister and J.R.'s lover, whom J.R. was framing for a prostitution charge? Bobby, who had been forced out of Southfork? Pamela, whose miscarriage had been caused by J.R.?

Everyone had a bone to pick with J.R.—even his mother, Miss Ellie, whose precious ranch had been mortgaged and whose sacred family unit had been dismantled by her eldest son. Las Vegas odds-makers began to solicit bets on the subject, and the response was so tremendous that city officials—perhaps fearing that the slot machines and craps tables were being neglected—declared that "Who shot J.R.?" was hands-off. "Dallas," they said, was "not an official sporting event," and besides, the answer to the question was known, if only to a few.

Once the assailant had been determined, only Katzman, Capice and a couple other individuals knew. Later, as the writing and filming began, the number grew to twenty, but stayed there. Even the cast was left in the dark, although Larry, Linda Gray and others had their pet theories.

Who didn't? Celebrities like Dan Rather and George Bush offered their guesses in print. Suggested Mike Connors, who played a detective in the TV series "Mannix," "I'd arrest the whole family and take away their charge accounts until somebody talked." Houston's famed criminal attorney Richard "Racehorse" Haynes not only had his theories, but offered to defend the assailant in court. And when Houston sheriff Jack Heard visited England over the summer, the British buttonholed him from the moment he stepped off the plane. "You're a sheriff from Texas," they said. "Who shot J.R.?"

Perhaps more than America, the usually demure England had flipped its wig over the controversy. Scotland Yard publicized its theories, and at least one British afficionado hired a private detective to solve the mystery. British college students threw J.R. disco parties and look-alike contests, and a middle-aged woman placed a transatlantic call to Parkland Hospital in Dallas. "How is J.R. doing?" she wanted to know.

Not that America wasn't in hysterics as well. In the dead heat of a presidential campaign, J.R. Ewing had stolen the show to the extent that both political parties got into the act. At a Dallas fundraiser, Jimmy Carter flashed his famous grin and said, "I came to Dallas to find out confidentially who shot J.R. If any of you could let me know that, I could finance the whole campaign this fall." Republicans, on the other hand, passed out buttons that read, "A Democrat Shot J.R."

Was the president above this silliness? Of course not. At a golf match in Las Vegas, Gerald Ford sidled up to Jim Davis and whispered, "You've got to tell me who shot J.R. or Betty's going to kill me."

Inevitably, a new candidate entered the fray. "J.R. for

President" bumper stickers, claimed one magazine, had outnumbered those for Carter and Ford. Hagman gleefully announced his platform: "When I'm elected, the first thing I'll do is raise the president's salary to $5 million because, you can't find the right guy to run a capitalist country for $200,000 a year. I mean, it's people after the buck who know how to run things, don't you agree? Then, after I get that straightened out, I will establish the Veterans for Future Wars. My idea is that government should pay for your education, set you up in business, give out all the GI benefits *before* there's war. Then, when a war comes, the forty-to fifty-year-olds, men *and* women, will be called to serve. 'Cause they're the ones who've gotten the benefits of the future war, right?"

As the day approached, security at the CBS studios tightened to the point of suffocation. The privileged few were sworn to absolute secrecy; the cast would not find out until the day of the show, at a cast party. Several scripts were written for the episode, each revealing a different criminal. On location, filmings were made of Cliff Barnes and Sue Ellen being taken into police custody. The network wasn't taking any chances.

Mere weeks before the telling season premiere, however, a thief made off with a copy of the script from Lorimar's MGM studio in Culver City, California. The culprit turned the document over to the *Los Angeles Herald-Examiner,* but the editors returned it to Lorimar without divulging its contents to the world. "Dallas" had dodged one last bullet.

And on Friday, September 19, Lorimar dispatched a world courier to London with a hand-carried videotape of the fateful episode, to be aired the following evening. At Heathrow Airport, the courier was taken to the BBC network's vault via a bulletproof van with a motorcycle escort. That evening, America would find out the identity of the attempted murderer, but Lorimar didn't want to spoil things for the British.

Between escargots and onion soup, Air France passengers bound for Europe were given the news courtesy of an air dispatcher. Throughout America, P.A. announcers at sparsely attended basketball games spread the word. And the phone lines lit up as fans from the East Coast spoiled it for their friends on the West Coast.

Sue Ellen had fingered her sister. Kristin had shot J.R.

As expected, the September 19 episode shattered all ratings precedents. Some 76 percent of all households had seen the show, breaking the series record set in 1967 for the last show of "The Fugitive"—breaking, in fact, the record for *any* entertainment program, dethroning the last installment of "Roots" in 1977. For the episode, the network had paid Lorimar a whopping $650,000. But CBS charged advertisers $500,000 a minute for commercials, almost double the going rate. That meant a tidy profit of $2,350,000.

Also as expected, the climactic scene had been up-staged by the circus-like atmosphere that preceded it. Critics and viewers complained that Kristin had been too obvious a choice, and the show lurched on for the next few episodes as if crippled by a hangover.

But "Dallas" stayed number one, despite the introduction of several clones. Already, CBS had instigated the Gary Ewing spin-off, "Knots Landing," in late 1979 with successful results. Now ABC and NBC came hustling into the fray. A month before the "Dallas" mystery-solver, NBC launched "Texas," a daytime soap set in Houston, and including not only the oil-rich but also the land-rich, communications-rich and Mideast-rich. They also released "Flamingo Road," an evening series set in Florida. Both floundered and were eventually canceled.

Also short-lived was yet another CBS series, the "Peyton Place"-ish "Secrets of Midland Heights," which lasted only a few months. But ABC eventually scored with "Dynasty," which debuted in January of 1981 and today surpasses "Dallas" in the weekly ratings on a frequent basis.

"Dallas," in the meantime, continued to enjoy immense success, but suffered slings and arrows for not matching its crowning achievement. The following season's cliffhanger—"Who is the woman at the bottom of the Southfork pool?"—not only failed to captivate the "Dallas" audience, but at least one critic announced that if you videotaped that particular episode and freeze-framed the scene where a blurred profile of the victim was shown, the identity was plain to see: it was Kristin, again.

Following the cliff-hanger, "Dallas" began its first summer of reruns. The ratings for them were a profound disappointment, and CBS executives found themselves explaining the awkward truth: "Dallas," like "Peyton Place" before it, had been seen so widely the first time around that viewers weren't compelled to tune in for the reruns. "Dallas" had become a victim of its own success.

Even the publicity had its counterproductive moments. Infuriated that *TV Guide* had prematurely leaked a key episode to the public, Lorimar president Lee Rich announced that the publication would no longer receive advance copies of the produce. Again, a clumsy scenario had emerged, as CBS was put in the position of demanding *less* publicity than the influential *TV Guide* wanted to give.

And J.R. Ewing made a poor showing in the presidential election, but the oilman kept a stiff upper lip. "I'm forward-thinking, honey, and that doesn't sit well with everybody," he told a reporter. No one knew this better than Larry Hagman, who had just witnessed a stampede of "forward-thinking" entrepreneurs cash in on the "Dallas" craze. They would continue to do so, and it wouldn't sit well with Larry.

CHAPTER NINE

Selling J.R.

The people who run Southfork Ranch can give their visitors just about anything except the answer to the question tourists most frequently ask: "Where's J.R.?" "They jokingly ask it," says Southfork general manager Ken Brixey, "but they really want to know. Everyone who comes here has this hope, somewhere in the back of their minds, of catching a glimpse of one of the Ewings."

Brixey understands this confusion of fantasy and reality, since for years he served as general manager of Elvis Presley's Graceland estate, one of the South's most popular tourist attractions. That the former Graceland general manager now works for Southfork is no coincidence. The goal of new ranch-owner Terry Trippet is for the "Dallas" commercial market to outlive the show itself, just as Graceland has kept on hoarding tourist dollars long after the King's death.

Fueling the J.R. fantasy is what Southfork is all about. Originally the property belonged to a man named, incredibly enough, J.R. Duncan. As part of the deal for shooting on Duncan Farms, Lorimar Productions gave Duncan exclusive worldwide marketing rights for products carrying the Southfork name. At the same time, tourists from all over the world began to show up at the Duncan doorstep, offering money for a look around the Ewing estate.

By 1980, the once-tranquil farm-to-market roads of Parker and Collin Counties screeched and roared with traffic. John and Susan Barber, neighbors of the Duncans who had fled the city in favor of the quiet rural life, took Southfork to court. The Barbers wanted an injunction that would halt filming at the ranch, since the tourist traffic had transformed the area into a demolition derby. A state district judge denied the injunction, and Southfork never looked back.

In 1984, Duncan sold the ranch to Tripett, a Dallas real-estate mogul with a penchant for quarter horses and Mercedes Benzes. Tripett would only say that the selling price was "eight figures." Immediately thereafter, the new Southfork owner pumped over a million dollars into renovating the ranch, intending to combine tourism and convention business on a scale never before attempted.

It's worked. Today, Southfork attracts more tourists than any other spot in Dallas. Over 40 percent of those tourists hail from other countries. Because the first 500 feet of the 167-acre spread finds itself in the city of Parker, where no retail business of any kind is allowed, tourists may walk this area for free. After that, it's five dollars to tour the Ewing household, and a gift shop teems with novelties ranging from "J.R. Mustard" (the J.R. is "just a coincidence," say the shop managers, since Southfork doesn't own rights to merchandise the "Dallas" characters) to one-inch square deeds of the Southfork property—a steal at ten dollars, which includes the mineral rights (although oil has never been found in Collin County).

In the meantime, the new Southfork convention center regularly hosts private parties, complete with J.R. Ewing look-alikes and country-western bands. For $2500, four couples may spend the night in the Southfork ranch house itself; upwards of $15,000 buys the whole ranch for a day, sans tourists. And in early 1986, Trippet ordered a feasibility study regarding the construction of—what else?—a Southfork Hotel.

Ken Brixey emphasizes that despite all the commercialism, Southfork is "still a working ranch," complete with horses and cattle. He admits that in this aspect, the ranch loses money, but painting the image of the Ewing property as a down-home Texas affair is a cosmetic necessity. And it's worked. "This place just prints money," Trippet says with a grin.

On television, courtesy of wide-angle shots, Southfork Ranch seems to sprawl forever. In reality, the property is no giant by Texas standards, and the mansion itself seems far too small for a family of normal folks who get along well, much less the feuding Ewings. (The swimming pool is barely the size of Larry's home Jacuzzi.) But somehow the mythical bigness of Southfork seems appropriate, since the commercial embrace of the J.R. fantasy has dwarfed the realities of "Dallas."

Larry Hagman held out for a new contract in 1980 because the fate of the TV show seemed to have been dumped squarely on his shoulders. Hardly a scene in the episodes existed in which J.R. did not appear, or else was discussed incessantly. Extra duties warranted extra pay. He got most of what he wanted, and pledged not to go back to the well again. (Actually, Larry's contract was again renegotiated in 1985, but without any fanfare or back-room arm-wrestling.)

But like everyone else associated with "Dallas," Larry cashed in on his fame as much as he could. "It's part of the game," he told *Playboy*. "Why deny yourself an opportunity that is going to be there only periodically, spasmodically? I may never get another chance like this in my lifetime. See, *everybody* takes advantage of the character, and the character is what I've developed. So if somebody is going to make $10 million off bumper stickers, T-shirts, posters, pins, coffee mugs, I'd be a damn fool if I didn't say, 'Hey, wait a minute, boys. I want a piece of that. It's *my* face on there.'"

But Larry didn't limit himself to J.R. propaganda. When a British jeans company offered him $230,000 to do a commercial, he didn't exactly shy away from the prospect. BVD Underwear also signed Larry to a commercial deal, and soon his schedule was bloated with paid public appearances and speaking engagements.

Unlike J.R., however, Larry seemed determined to retain his human perspective. "I'll tell you, I feel compassion for the rich," he quipped, "now that I'm one of them." In New York, Larry continued to wear a ten-gallon hat and accept kisses from women, and in Dallas he continued to let the top down on his convertible and cruise through the city, waving and yee-hawing with "Flight of the Valkyries" blaring from his car speakers. The ugly downside of success seemed to have momentarily spared Larry Hagman—or more to the point, he refused to be imprisoned by it.

Others in the cast didn't fare quite as well. Cathy Lee Crosby's stock as an actress rose considerably once the news broke that her character, Kristin Shepherd, had been J.R.'s attacker. Subsequently, the daughter of Bing Crosby signed a lucrative contract for a lead in a series called "Golden Globe" and left "Dallas" five episodes after shooting J.R. Predictably, "Golden Globe" flopped.

More recently, Patrick Duffy left the role of Bobby Ewing after the 1984 season, complaining that Bobby had become a dimensionless do-gooder, while J.R. and the others had blossomed as unsavory types. Larry publicly voiced his disappointment that Lorimar and Duffy couldn't work something out, but others in the cast felt little sympathy for the actor. "There was a time when I felt my character had become too passive, passive to the point where I lost respect for her," said Victoria Principal. "So I went to the producers, and we worked on it. The producers aren't my enemies. They've always been willing to listen."

And as Ken Kercheval pointed out, "It's how you interpret the character that makes the difference." But Duffy obviously felt differently, and left the cast for more satisfying territory. He even went so far as to state that "Dallas" had become a "tired" concept and that he would never return.

But the former "Man From Atlantis"—which also starred Alan Fudge and Belinda Montgomery, two actors who haven't found steady work since the series was canceled—had to swallow his words. The best he could do was play a goat on *Alice in Wonderland* and a rapist on "Hotel." Fortunately for Duffy, "Dallas" experienced a ratings decline in his absence, and so the return of Bobby Ewing on May 16, 1986 could be viewed by the actor as his saving of a damsel in distress.

The show had, in fact, suffered from the death of Bobby Ewing if not the departure of Duffy. After the death of Jock Ewing (necessitated by the death of actor Jim Davis), J.R. remarked to Sue Ellen, "You and me and Bobby and Mama are the only family left." The viewers couldn't help but agree. On October of 1984, in fact, Bar-

bara Bel Geddes had stepped down from the Miss Ellie role to undergo heart surgery. Her replacement, Donna Reed, did not appease the viewers, and she unsuccessfully filed a $7.5-million breach-of-contract suit against the show upon being fired in April of 1985 and replaced by the recuperated Geddes.

Now with Duffy gone, "Dallas" began to depend more and more on actors outside the original cast and Ewing core: Howard Keel, playing Miss Ellie's new husband; Priscilla Presley, yet another beautiful ex-wife of Bobby; Steve Kanaly, whose long-standing Ray Krebbs character, along with his wife Donna (played by Susan Howard), gained more play upon discovering that Ray was Jock Ewing's son by previous marriage; and multitudes of Ewing love interests, business partners and alleged relatives. By killing off Bobby, the producers completely abandoned the original story line for the miniseries, and had removed the appealing tension between Bobby and J.R.

Other cast problems surfaced. Sue Ellen's drinking problem had finally lowered her to bag-lady status, to Linda Gray's complete lack of amusement. J.R., in Larry's words, had become "too nice," and in fact several episodes contained countless references to "the new J.R." as opposed to the nasty older model. While the Ewings paled with predictability, the Barneses flourished. Kercheval's small-minded loser, Cliff, upstaged J.R. in more ways than just money, and Principal's Pamela began to grow out of the Little Miss Perfect mold and develop a sort of cool-headed believability.

Nothing seemed the same after the shooting episode. But perhaps the most unsettling change had been the convergence of dollar-mongers from the moment Kristin Sheperd took aim at J.R. Typical of the quick-kill entrepreneurs was Nathanial W. Parker III, who began to sell phony stock for Ewing Land, Oil & Cattle Co. for "a real bargain," six dollars a share. Hoping that consumers would buy the stocks for their worst enemies, Parker's product contained the fine print, "Partner, you've just been had by J.R."

Under the pseudonym Lee Raintree, Con Sellers had written a novel based on the first five episodes of "Dallas." Leaden with Texas stereotypes, the commissioned novel nonetheless sold a staggering 400,000 copies.

Even established businesses got into the act. San Antonio's Pearl Brewing Company announced in the middle of 1980 that it was introducing a new beer, J.R. Ewing's Private Stock—sold in cans on which was written, "If you have to ask how much my beer costs, you probably can't afford it."

"A man will buy J.R. Ewing's Private Stock because it says a lot about him without him even opening his mouth," said brewery vice president Frank Spinosa, perhaps unaware of the irony. He added, "People today buy an image, not a beer. This beer will do well as long as the television show does well." In fact, said Spinosa, Pearl had already received orders for a half-million cases within the first week, had obtained the marketing rights to the other principal "Dallas" characters and was looking into the possibility of marketing a nonalcoholic version in Arab countries.

Like Pearl's infamous Billy Beer (named after Jimmy Carter's beer-swilling brother), J.R. Ewing's Private Stock eventually died on the shelves for one very good reason: people didn't like the way it tasted. Similarly, people stopped buying J.R. dolls and J.R. playing cards, stopped rubbing on the J.R. body talc and J.R. cologne, and stopped reading the "Dallas" comic strip. (People never got a chance to stop using J.R. Ewing toilet paper or J.R.

kitchen sponges, since Lorimar didn't approve for trade-marking those particular brainstorms.)

But the selling of J.R. had its loftier moments. A popular T-shirt proclaimed, "Will Rogers never met J.R." Macy's opened J.R. boutiques in their New York and London stores. In 1985, an album calling itself *"Dallas": The Music Story* hit the record racks. Included was the soon-to-be-hit single "J.R.! Who Do You Think You Are," performed by former singer and current husband of Miss Ellie, Howard Keel. Between cracking whips, Keel intoned lines like, "Now some would say he wasn't born, he was hatched from a lizard's spleen; with a talent for doing a dirty deed that would turn a rattler green."

But as the goose that laid the golden egg lost its magic, so did the peripheral profits begin to dry up. Larry's once-obsessive bid to reel in merchandising revenues relaxed when it became apparent that the world no longer craved a closetful of J.R. dolls.

Of course, the show's decline in popularity was hardly a shock—not only because "Dallas" couldn't possibly sustain the fever pitch accompanying the J.R. shooting, but also because no show lasts forever. Once-indestructible series like "The Mary Tyler Moore Show" finally fizzled out; even critical darlings like "Hill Street Blues" find themselves deserted by the formerly faithful. Of greater concern to those associated with "Dallas" is the programming trend away from *all* serials, and the now widely held belief that such shows have exhausted viewer interest.

Yet "Dallas" continues to nestle itself in the Nielsen top ten, where it's been for seven eventful years. When people accost Larry Hagman on the street, they still call him "J.R.," kiss him or shake his hand, call him a rascal and watch admiringly as he walks away. "Dallas" is still "Dallas," frothing with greed and incest and betrayal and terrifying ambition.

And the show still belongs to J.R. Ewing. "The show can go as long as Larry doesn't get bored," declared Howard Keel. "He is *the* man."

Out in Southfork, the myth intends to outlive the man. Despite the show's ratings decline, tourism at Southfork doubled in 1985 and is expected to double again in 1986. "Dallas" may see its last episode in a couple of years, acknowledges Terry Trippet, but reruns and delayed telecasts overseas may keep 'em coming for . . . decades? Who knows?

Trippet does, or thinks he does. He didn't pay eight figures for a quick kill. The day he visited Southfork, he also telephoned the Ponderosa Ranch, filming site of the TV series "Bonanza." Filming had ceased since 1972, he learned, yet over a decade later, as many as 500,000 tourists a year clamored for a sight of the famous ranch.

The next day, Terry Trippet bought Southfork from J.R. Duncan. He doubtless felt as Larry had; "I may never get another chance like this in my lifetime."

CHAPTER TEN

Dateline: Malibu

We're so glad Larry is playing such a bad character. It means that when he comes home he has to be extra nice.

—Mary Martin

Like Weatherford, the colony that Larry Hagman now calls home is a small and tightly knit community of people who cherish their privacy and the great outdoors. Otherwise, Malibu and Weatherford are about as much alike as Peter Pan and J.R. Ewing.

The twenty-six-mile beach strip has been called "the ghetto of the rich," and with good reason. Ever since Vitagraph moved to the West Coast and opened its studios in 1911, Hollywood has been the site of the movie industry; but as an escape from the tortuous L.A. smog and unholy trappings of the Beverly Hills lifestyle, movie heavyweights have long designated Malibu as their bedroom community. Despite the opulence one might expect from celebrity dwellings, many of the houses are packed closely together along the beach, ghetto style. Everyone wants a slice of Paradise Pie, it seems, but there's only so much to go around.

Long before the invention of the surfboard, Malibu was a settlement for the Chumash Indians until the Spaniards chased them off. In 1887, however, upscale Harvard graduate Frederick Hastings Rindge bought the entire 17,000-acre colony. Rindge died in 1905, but his wife, May, took over and soon became known as the Queen of the Malibu. May Rindge's disdain for all things industrial led to her hiring dozens of armed henchmen who patrolled the property and chased off would-be traders. The barricade effectively cut off the commercial flow between San Francisco and Los Angeles, and the ensuing war between California merchants and the Queen of the Malibu was rumored to have been a bloody one.

Before the depression, the Rindge estate had been worth an obscene $100 million. By 1938, though, the fight to seal off Malibu from the outside world had led May to financial ruin. With just enough money left to build a castle on a hill behind Malibu Creek, the Rindge widow led her last years there in bitter seclusion.

As early as 1927, however, May had leased a sliver of her land to silent-screen star Anna Q. Nilsson. Soon to follow were W.C. Fields, Greta Garbo, Tyrone Power, Cary Grant, Barbara Stanwyck and anybody else worth mentioning in Hollywood. The celebrity floodgates had opened.

Thus did Malibu become everything May Rindge held in contempt: a crowded, expensive magnet for what she might consider indecency. Her castle was sold to Franciscan monks and later found its use as a monastic retreat for overworked businessmen. Casinos and houses of ill repute sprang up on the beach, converting the area to what came to be known as "the Gold Coast."

By the sixties the gambling and prostitution was gone,

105

but a whole new scene had replaced it. After visiting Malibu, Rex Reed wrote: "For nine months of the year, this ugly little collection of motels and empty Coke bottles looks like any other boring retirement center marked by a bright flag on a Medicare map. Then comes June and it all starts happening. The movie stars and jet-set buddhas pack up their sneakers, their coconut oil, their Martini mixers, their poodles and all the kids from all their previous marriages, and head for the sea, descending on Malibu like sand crabs in their blue jeans and Yves St. Laurent chain belts. Then for as long as the summer lasts, they get stoned on pot, barbeque everything but the delivery boys from Western Union, and work like hell to make their summer rent money pay off."

Malibu developed the reputation as a sin city for the elite—a place, it has been written, "where you lie on the sand and look at the stars, or vice versa." In 1983, the television series "Malibu" reduced the colony's image to coke spoons and orgies. The series didn't last, but the rap goes on.

It's a bad rap, actually. People of substantial wealth, like Larry Hagman, may live here; but like Larry, they raise families, not coca leaves. And in at least one way, Malibu is still as May Rindge would have preferred it: isolated, or at least semi-isolated. The colony has no airport, and the train passes through but does not stop. On the other hand, its main strip—the Pacific Coast Highway—is an extension of the Santa Monica Freeway, which means that Hollywood employees can commute to the studios without having to endure a maze of one-lane roads.

The ties that bind the Malibu community are not simply professional. Few would imagine life here as one fraught with peril, yet natural disasters always seem imminent. In 1982, a furious storm flung mud and logs through Dyan Cannon's glass doors. In 1978, the house of Burgess Meredith fell into the Pacific during a torrential rain. A year later, a similar downpour prompted then-governor Edmund Brown to declare Malibu a disaster area. (At the time, his girlfriend, Linda Ronstadt, lived on the beach.) The storms caused tremendous vegetation growth, and in the ensuing hot months, the plants would dry completely. Result: the brush fires of 1979, similar to those in the sixties that had reduced dozens of Malibu homes to ashes.

In 1983, ocean gales ruined or partially destroyed hundreds of Malibu dwellings, including Barbra Streisand's pink-and-green "easter egg" house and the infamous spread that Billie Jean King repossessed from her lover. As in other years, neighbors banded together and lent a helping hand. Some, like Ronstadt and Rod Stewart, tired of the earthquakes, mud slides and storms, and moved out of Malibu. But for many other stars, the chance that the San Andreas Fault will one day inspire the deliverance of Malibu into the Pacific Ocean is a chance they'll have to take. You endure the rough with the smooth in Paradise.

The Hagmans have lived here since moving from Manhattan during the "I Dream of Jeannie" days. Larry also owns property in New Mexico and travels a great deal, but for him Malibu will always be home. It may seem incongruous that a gregarious Texan who enjoys pressing the flesh with the public prefers the isolated beach life to one in say, New York.

But Larry has learned, as a matter of self-preservation, to ration his exposure to the outside world. The demands of "Dallas" don't allow for much leisure, and what free time he does accumulate is usually spent at home. That's by choice. Given a choice, he would rather be with his family.

LARRY HAGMAN

Larry and Maj have now been married for thirty-two years. He attributes that to spending as much time together as possible. It's likely that the importance of togetherness was a lesson learned in his childhood: Mary and Ben Hagman seemed destined to travel in different directions, from the moment Ben dropped his new bride off at the Nashville finishing school to the moment Mary made her first trip to California.

In Larry's profession, of course, marriages tend to melt under the bright lights of fame. Larry gets thousands of letters weekly, and most are from women. "When I did 'I Dream of Jeannie,' I never did get any sexually oriented mail," he said. "Let me tell you, that has changed dramatically." Women continue to kiss him and slip him suggestive notes in public. But even at the height of Larry's international popularity, during the who-shot-J.R. saga, Larry and Maj traveled everywhere together. "We're partners on this trip," Larry has said of life with Maj, and nothing seems likely to change that.

Coping with Larry's stardom has been made easier for Maj by the fact that her own career is in high gear. As a designer of Jacuzzis, she has constructed handsome spas for a number of her Malibu neighbors, and for a tidy fee. But Maj's crowning achievement is the hot tub that is the centerpiece of the Hagmans' newly renovated home. The enormous tub (which includes a Jacuzzi, naturally) lies between the Hagmans' living room and the beach; it's ten feet by ten feet, about five-feet deep, and comfortably holds up to six people.

The spa is only part of the massive renovation the Hagmans did on their house a few years ago. Noticing that the wooden house was rotting and that the termites were taking over, the Hagmans took the opportunity to reshape the house with personal touches. Literally designing the plans around Maj's L-shaped spa, what the

Hagmans came up with was an astounding adobe structure that combines practicality with luxury. Among the features in the two-story house are eight fireplaces hand-sculpted by Maj, wall art by their son-in-law, four bedrooms with hydraulic beds, brick floors, solar-heated water, a swimming pool and an array of television and video equipment. Since Larry directs "Dallas" occasionally, he prefers state-of-the-art equipment that is also portable so it can be used for scouting locations. All told, his video equipment—a three-quarter-inch recorder, two one-half-inch recorders for dubbing purposes, a quarter-inch Betamax and a small technicolor unit—is all that's needed for industry-quality productions.

In Larry's home office, each window faces the ocean—which actually laps at the door during rough weather. Two seven-foot steer horns adorn one wall, and flanking them are bookcases filled with issues of *National Geographic* dating back to 1924. (He is a fiend for this publication, and frequently scurries off to garage sales in search of ancient back issues.) On another wall is a picture of Jim Davis, his father on "Dallas"—a man Larry had been extremely fond of.

The California Highway Patrol office flanks one side of the Hagman home. Their neighbor on the other side is Burgess Meredith, a friend of Larry's for years. Their friendship nearly dissolved, however, during the construction of the Hagmans' new home in 1982. Meredith felt that the additions were blocking his view of the beach, and he eventually sued Larry over the matter. Meredith lost and considered the possibility of building a wall between the two houses. When asked if he would have a mural painted on the wall, Meredith replied, "What I think I'll paint is a view of what the view would be if Larry's home weren't there."

LARRY HAGMAN

Larry doesn't go to parties much. Whether he's in Dallas or the MGM studios in Culver City, California, filming scenes of "Dallas" can drag on for up to twelve to sixteen hours a day. He prefers to awaken before dawn, drive to work while dictating "Dallas" dialogue on his portable tape recorder, then return home for dinner and a swim. Larry has said that by ten—whether he's at home or at a party—he begins to nod off.

But frequently the Hagmans have dinner guests, sometimes twenty or so at a time. Who is invited and what is served usually depends on who's in town—Juanita Hagman from Weatherford or Mary Martin from San Francisco, Phillip Mengel or Carroll O'Connor from New York. Unlike other Malibu dinner parties, the Hagmans' affairs aren't manditorily star-studded. Sometimes the guests are celebrities, but just as many are not, like the man who owns a meat market in Michigan whom Larry met while on location for "I Dream of Jeannie." People who briefly walk into the Hagmans' lives, like the construction workers who renovated their house, find themselves at these dinner parties, chatting lightly with J.R. Ewing.

Frequently the hosts and guests adjourn to the hot tub. If "Monday Night Football" is on, they'll splash around and watch the action on the nearby screen. Larry far prefers football talk to the political conversations O'Connor favors. He also prefers that these sessions take place without bothering with swimsuits, although "Carroll and Nancy O'Connor never do things like that," he has said.

Occasionally the Hagmans will throw a party; these, too, aren't typical celebrity bashes. A couple of years ago, Larry invited fifty members of the press to his house—an unusual gesture, except that Larry has a number of good friends in the news media. As many as two-hundred fifty people have fit semi-comfortably in the new adobe house, but Larry and Maj enjoy smaller gatherings, where they can demonstrate their considerable cooking skills and maintain the relaxed atmosphere for which the house was clearly intended.

Instead of utilizing the customary social mechanisms, Larry Hagman has chosen to mingle with the Malibu community in a striking manner: he throws parades. Structurally and in every other way, the parades are not confined to any particular regimen. They're simply Larry's way of showing Malibu his idea of a good time, and inviting them to join in.

The parades usually, but not always, take place at three o'clock on weekend afternoons. Labor Day is a good excuse for throwing a parade, as is the Fourth of July; on the other hand, so is the anniversary of the release of the Pentagon Papers to the *New York Times*.

The parades began during the Vietnam days, coinciding with the heaviest flurry of protests across the nation. Recalled Peter Fonda, one of Larry's closest friends, "Everybody was on their deck as we went by, wanting to know what we were protesting about. 'Shitfire!' Larry would call out, 'We're not protesting anything. Just get down here and march!' Larry would start playing the flute or banging the drum. He was demonstrating for life and parading for fun. There was no reason to parade. The purpose was just to do it."

Sometimes the parades consist only of Larry, Maj and a couple of friends. At other times, neighbors like Dyan Cannon join in, and it's not rare for upwards of a hundred locals and beach bums to join in. Larry usually takes the lead, playing his flute (which he does quite skillfully) and marching along in a gorilla suit, karate uniform or Indian regalia, along with various medals. The costumes and medals are chosen at random and signify absolutely nothing other than Larry's whims.

The parades are Larry Hagman's contribution to Malibu. In this unorthodox manner, he says to his image-conscious community: Loosen up! Be ridiculous! Dare to goof off in public, with the public! It is the sort of message that the colony's Hollywood stars could stand to hear several times a day. Many of them have less to lose than the star of "Dallas," but Larry's refusal to be jailed by his fame doesn't begin and end with eating out in public or doing his own driving. He chooses his own friends and his own ways of interacting with the outside world.

No behavioral creed will prevent Larry Hagman from marching in the California sand in an Indian headdress, like the Chumash tribes did hundreds of years before him.

It took Maj awhile before she felt comfortable enough to parade with her husband. "He'd always been a bit of a show-off, and for years I wanted to sort of sneak off and hide," she said. "Preston *really* used to shy away, embarrassed, especially when Larry would put on one of his many gorilla suits."

But now Maj marches, and so do the Hagmans' two children. It's clear that Larry's belief about a close family isn't limited to his wife. The Hagmans, parents and children, follow the dictum that the family that stays together, stays together.

Larry avoids talking about the travails of his childhood, insisting that it was adventurous and that he was always in some family member's loving care. Nonetheless, his early years bear scant resemblance to the manner in which he and Maj have raised their children.

"We've moved a lot," said Larry, "and whenever we had to go someplace, we'd pick up the kids and take them out of school. They grew up sleeping in bathtubs, closets, you name it, but they were always with us. Now they're well-adjusted, interesting children."

Recalled Larry, "When they were younger I always took them out of school to go on tour with me or to Europe, because I figured that the travel was worth more than the school. Of course," he laughed, "they can't read or write, but they sure do know how to travel."

Both have inherited their father's independence, and have forged their own paths with minimal assistance from Larry. When Preston turned sixteen, Larry cut off the boy's allowance to encourage him to work. Preston responded by getting a job as a grocery-store bag-boy, and then later became a waiter.

Preston, named after his great-grandfather the Weatherford judge, decided against law and acting at an early age. His passion, like grandmother Mary's, was to be able to fly. The tall (about six-feet-four), curly-headed Hagman therefore enrolled in Northrop University as an aerospace-engineering student and obtained his commercial pilot's license. In the summer of 1985, his wife, Starla, gave birth to their first child, Mary Noel, and Larry became a grandfather at the age of fifty-four.

Like Ben and Larry, father and son have always enjoyed taming the wilderness together. They don't hunt that much anymore since, as Larry has said, "I don't like to kill anything. But I do like fishing. I suppose fish experience pain, too, but then, who gives a shit?"

On the other hand, the relationship between Heidi (who now goes by the name Kristina) and Larry contains a few vague similarities to that between Mary and Larry. By high school, Kristina had decided that she, too, would like to carry on the family acting tradition. At the age of fifteen, she began a catering service with a school friend and made $3000, which financed a trip to Europe. The

113

following year she studied dance therapy at San Francisco State, and supported herself with jobs as a model, a cook in a vegetarian restaurant and a janitor at the local art academy.

When the time came to start nosing around for acting jobs, Larry helped Kristina as Mary had helped him. The rosy-cheeked blonde landed two cameo appearances as a receptionist in "Dallas," and later Carroll O'Connor signed her up as Linda, the waitress in "Archie Bunker's Place."

Since that time, Kristina's interest in acting has waned slightly, and she's chosen to concentrate primarily on painting. She also married fellow artist Brian Blount, whose works, as previously noted, can be found in the house of his in-laws.

Malibu Mission. Larry Hagman's house goes by that name—or sometimes Mission: Malibu, or perhaps Fort Malibu. Indeed, the edifice is the mission wherein Larry practices his eccentric rituals, as will be detailed in the next chapter.

But the house is more than Larry's laboratory of idiosyncrasies. In many ways, Malibu Mission embodies the traits that have kept Maj and Larry happily together since 1954—a feat that Larry has acknowledged as being "some kind of record in Hollywood." They conceived it and even played a major role in the building of it. The house suits them, and not just because it contains a great stereo and a ton of TV screens. The house is large, but it's also modest in many ways. The walls aren't littered with rare artworks, and the wood used in Larry's office is from crate boxes. The furniture is stylish but hardly garish; it seems to have been selected to emphasize comfort rather than as a statement of wealth.

The parades on Malibu Beach are for the community,

for whoever has the nerve to join in. Malibu Mission, however, is for the Hagman family. In ways that May Rindge, the Queen of the Malibu, would surely have approved of, Larry regards the sanctity of his family as one that nothing shall violate.

"There is only one thing that ever would cause me to become physically violent," Larry told an interviewer. "And that is if anyone should ever, in word or action, threaten my wife or my children. Of these people whom I love, *I am very, very protective.*"

Barring such a violation, the parade continues.

CHAPTER ELEVEN

Larry Hagman: A Global Mythology

The preceding chapters have hopefully made two things clear: first, that there *is* a J.R. Ewing within Larry Hagman. J.R. is a creation of memories and behavioral traits, and one of which Larry is exceedingly fond, but secondly, that Larry Hagman is *not* J.R. Ewing. Both points seem obvious enough, but it's easy to lose sight of where fact and fantasy vanish and reappear.

Larry likes to say that J.R. does what he does so as to "take care of his business and his family." In those matters, actor and character are kindred spirits, in light of Larry's contract battle and protectiveness toward his family. But J.R. wants everyone else's money in addition to his own, and his sense of family indicates a fondness for tradition rather than for the people who sit at his dinner table.

Like the rest of the world, Larry seems to admire J.R. Ewing, albeit grudgingly. As the eighties began, *Esquire* pointed to J.R. as a likely hero of the decade—a man who is "mean, effective, revels in his freedom." Like no one in real life, J.R. Ewing can walk through the shimmering towers of Dallas' other-worldly Central Business District without fear that the modern world will shackle him. Like Ben Hagman's oil buddies, J.R. is a master of the brutal Texas turf, a man much closer to the soil than to civilization. But unlike the colorful Weatherford characters, J.R. also knows how to stay on top in the eighties, how to manipulate minds in the computer age. He is a man out of time, but just in time for us.

So is Larry Hagman, who possesses a certain boldness of character that masks as goofiness. Even by the standards of his industry, Larry is something of an oddity. The "Dallas" cast has come to cherish his costumes and stunts, particularly on those sweltering afternoons in Southfork when tempers are short.

Larry admits that he likes to show off—a trait his stepmother terms "typical Hagman." But what he's showing off is not just the freedom that success brings ("I'm famous, I can do what I want"), but also the freedom *from* success. This level of frontier individualism has J.R. beat, since the Ewing Oil boss doesn't know when to draw the line—when to call it quits and relax.

Larry does. There is a flag that flies above Malibu Mission, a blue-and-yellow sheet decorated with two hearts, two classic comedy masks and the words, "Vita Celebratio Est." The Latin words translate as "Life is a celebration." Not a contest, not a bitch, not a jungle, not a dress rehearsal. A *celebration*.

"Vita Celebratio Est" is a Hagman creed. So is the aphorism which faces Larry every morning on his bathroom mirror: "Don't worry. Be happy. Feel good." The first two sentences resulted from his psychotherapy sessions during the "I Dream of Jeannie" struggles. Larry added the last sentence late—an acknowledgment that physical health leads to mental health.

As J.R. Ewing became larger than life to millions of viewers in 1979, Larry also became larger—much larger. He ballooned up to 222 pounds—a result, he later said, of "eating my own cooking: chicken pastille, chili, beef bourgignon and the best spaghetti in Malibu." So while J.R. recovered in a Dallas hospital, Larry and Maj both dedicated much of 1980 to shedding the excess tonnage. They gave the commercially marketed Opti-Fast diet a try, which involved eating almost no food, shunning alcohol and, instead, living off of three daily-prescribed packages of powder that contained egg whites, skim milk, and other ingredients. During that time, Larry had his blood checked weekly to make sure that he wasn't in danger of malnutrition, and he hit the sack by ten o'clock.

It sounds excruciating, but the results were impressive: Larry lost thirty-two pounds in thirty-six days during that period, and Maj lost forty-two pounds in sixty-seven days. Today, the six-foot-tall Hagman hovers around a svelte 180 pounds.

It isn't easy to stay slim as a television star—not only because the temptations are abundant, but also because the schedules can be brutal, and they leave little time for exercise and careful dietary planning. When Larry directed episodes of "Knots Landing," for example, his schedule looked something like this: Get to "Dallas" set by seven in the morning; shoot four or five pages of script; have lunch with Maj; drive over to the "Knots Landing" set and do about five more pages of script; and call it a day at one in the morning.

Even when not directing "Knots Landing," Larry drives to the "Dallas" studio by seven, studying his lines via tape recorder along the way. He's home again by six or so, at which point he takes a shower, takes off his makeup and greases his face to keep his pores clean. Larry might then mix a wine spritzer, rifle through the day's mail ("discarding anything," he told a reporter, "that makes me unhappy"), take a Jacuzzi and then build a fire on the beach. By that time it's around 8:00, and Maj has made him some soup or Japanese salad. By 9:30, he's asleep.

To stay in shape, Larry does most of his exercising in the morning. He runs two miles on the beach, then sometimes swims in his pool—with a rope tying him to the end of the pool behind him and the poolside television on, "so it doesn't get boring." He also works out three times a week in his room, using a portable gym that weighs about seventy pounds.

Larry occasionally treats himself to liquor and barbeque, but for the most part he sticks to the strict limitations of his diet. "We're vegetarians, you know," he said. "People don't trust that. They'd rather you were a gangster than a vegetarian."

Larry has said that when he was about sixteen years old, he found himself alone with a Weatherford girl—a chance, he figured, for some good old-fashioned sex education. The girl struck a bargain with him. She would let him touch her breast if he smoked one of her cigarettes.

Young Larry eagerly accepted the terms. Sixteen years later, however, he was still smoking cigarettes. Then came the damning surgeon general's report linking tobacco to lung cancer, and on that very day Larry Hagman put down his pack for good.

"I quit when I realized how destructive it is to your body," Larry later said. But what distressed him was that so many other people, including his close friends, continued to puff away their lives as if the surgeon general had said nothing. He joined the American Cancer Society in a role as chairman, which had usually been purely ceremonial. But Larry appeared in commercials on television, made speeches, and became the director for the Anti-

119

Smoking Campaign that included the "adopt-a-smoker" brainstorm of helping friends quit.

As always, Larry tries to maintain a sense of humor about a subject that is of very solemn interest to him. Almost wherever he goes, Larry carries with him a portable, battery-operated fan made in Japan. The fan serves to blow smoke back into the smoker's face—a gag, but one with a point. Back at Malibu Mission, plaques can be found throughout the house, gently asking guests not to smoke inside. The chief offender, it has been said, is the cigar-puffing Carroll O'Connor, although Juanita Hagman also has been banished to the balcony.

In some cases, Larry's nagging has paid off. He coaxed Jim Davis into quitting his three-pack-a-day habit (Davis, incidentally, did *not* die of lung cancer), and then set to work on Victoria Principal and Barbara Bel Geddes. Neither of his children smokes.

Larry finds it difficult to have respect for people who put something between them and Larry's "Feel good" principle. "If these people, these smokers, realize what they are doing," Larry said, "then you must have less respect for them. They're losers. Take Alexander Haig. This man smokes four packs of cigarettes a day. Now, how can you trust a man like that?"

During the late sixties, Larry had spent a number of days as Major Anthony Nelson, the man with the genie named Jeannie. On one particular episode, the script called for an inordinate amount of hollering. The next day, Larry realized he had lost his voice, and the doctor prescribed twenty-four hours of silence.

As it turned out, Larry enjoyed the treatment immensely. Life took on a different perspective: silence was peaceful, and not talking forced him to listen to others more. At rock bottom, it was a fascinating discipline. Already Larry had developed a fondness for meditation, and later for rigorous exercise and fastidious dieting.

From that point onward, Larry began a new practice: silent Sundays. Preston and Kristina have learned a sign language so they can communicate with their father on these days. Good friends know not to call the Hagman house on Sunday, unless they can handle Larry's accepted mode of response: whistling. "His family and close friends know the tone of Larry's idiosyncrasies," said Peter Fonda. And in fact, Larry will modulate his whistles to indicate doubt, excitement, confusion, thoughtfulness and joy. But a more distant associate might feel a greater sense of alienation when calling Malibu Mission on a Sunday and hearing a series of cryptic whistles on the other end of the line.

The silence, in fact, has gotten Larry into trouble more than once. When traveling, for example, Maj has had trouble explaining to immigration and customs officials why her husband refuses to answer their questions.

On another occasion, Mary Martin threw a party at her Palm Springs home and invited several distinguished guests—among them Walter Annenburg, a former ambassador and currently the owner and publisher of *TV Guide*, the most influential periodical in the business. Annenburg had been anxious to meet the new star of "Dallas," and seemed quite unamused when Larry merely smiled as a response to the publisher's questions. Mary had to do some fast explaining, before Annenburg lost his temper.

Larry engages in these disciplines as a liberating experience. But disciplines for many people can become ends unto their own, and thus ultimately imprison those who practice them. Perhaps this is why Larry occasionally breaks his silent-Sunday code, just as he makes exceptions to his dietary habits. When Juanita takes the flight from

Texas to visit, for example, he won't subject her to whistles. And, said Larry, "There was the time I sliced my toe on a rock and I called out some four-letter words."

There was also the time when Larry invited a host of TV critics over to Malibu Mission for a party and interview session. It was a Sunday, but Larry was talkative—a concession, perhaps, to the fact that "Dallas" needed a ratings boost.

Larry's relationship with the media has chilled slightly over the last few years. As a measure of self-preservation, he no longer grants the press the instant access to him they enjoyed in 1980. In fact, he now refuses to do any interviews with TV reporters unless the subject is exclusively Larry rather than "Dallas" or one of its other characters. He also will not work on the set until all photographers have been cleared from the premises.

It's not that Larry has now decided that he doesn't need the media or that reporters are without exception contemptible creatures. More to the point, his familiarity to millions of people has forced him to draw certain lines to protect his privacy, and he has had to face the fact that some elements within the media are unwholesome. Reports in different tabloids that Larry drinks on the "Dallas" set, that he loses his temper constantly, that he still cannot get along with his famous mother and other untruths have infuriated him. He has said that he would consider filing suit, except that lawsuits only make lawyers rich.

Instead, Larry has said to a number of reporters, he'd like to get even with sleazy journalists by doing a movie called *Vendetta, Inc.* The movie would star Hagman as a tabloid publisher who gets his in the end, and would drag out a number of skeletons in the unscrupulous publisher's closet in the process.

It seems unlikely that Larry will ever sink his teeth into

this particular project—not only because he continues to stay busy, but because for the most part the press has been quite good to him. It's a two-way street, of course: Hagman is an engaging interviewee, an eccentric with a realistic view of daily reporters. "The press is always there anyway," he said once while defending his decision to do interviews. "It's their job to find out something. So what's the difference? At least if they have a chance to know you, they might be a little kinder. They might print part of the truth."

For the most part, the news media has recognized Larry for what he is: a rare professional who has made it to the top on the basis of talent and a few slivers of luck, and one who has few illusions about what the world owes him. And among a few news writers (particularly those from Texas), Larry has developed friendships as close as any of his others.

Over the years, Larry has also deemed it necessary to moderate his encouragement of fans. For a long time, he would spend hours signing autographs on the street; later, he passed out his phony J.R. $100 bills.

Eventually, he decided to give autographs only after the requester satisfied Larry's demands. "I'm a firm believer that anything you get for nothin' loses value," he told one reporter, "so I tell them, 'You've got to pay for this.' When they ask what, I say, 'A poem, a prayer or a song.'"

This approach has seemed the only way to keep the autograph hunters at bay. ("Mostly they're women," Larry has said. "Age eight to eighty, they hit on me, sometimes in groups of 600. It's like sharks feeding.") "Normally, if it's only one person, I ask him to recite some verse from a poem or tell a story or say one hundred Hail Marys," he said. Larger groups often find themselves singing for a signature. On one occasion in Dallas, several autograph hunters reluctantly began a round of "Row Row Row Your Boat," then continued with renewed gusto as the entire "Dallas" cast joined in.

These days, Larry usually refuses to sign autographs on the street. His fondness for attention and for attracting crowds has been tempered by an incident in 1984, when both he and Linda Gray were persistently followed by a young man all summer long. Both eventually hired bodyguards and switched rented residences.

In a fascinating interview with *Playboy* in 1980, Larry Hagman illustrated the political differences between J.R. and Larry. For example, J.R. would have left the American hostages in Iran, since they took a risk working overseas to begin with. Larry, on the other hand, would be inclined to do almost whatever it took to get the hostages back to the States.

Other differences surfaced in the interview. It's unlikely, for example, that J.R. would ever try LSD, although Larry did on a number of occasions during the "I Dream of Jeannie" days, concluding that the experience was "just about the best thing that ever happened to me." It's also doubtful that the two share the same views on presidential politics. "Do I get involved in politics?" Larry said. "Yeah, I give a thousand dollars to the Republican Party, a thousand to the Democrats. I'm a member of the Peace and Freedom Party myself. During Vietnam, they were for getting us the heck out of there."

And Larry claims that he has voted for Dr. Benjamin Spock three elections in a row, on the grounds that "Any man who openly admits having messed up two generations, he's got my vote."

For the most part, Larry prefers to keep his politics to himself. It would seem, though, that while sharing J.R.'s disdain for bureaucrats and mounting taxation, the actor has a charitable side that would baffle the Ewing millionaire. Beyond his efforts to curb the nation's smoking habits, Larry has also made a government film that calls for the deinstitutionalization of the mentally retarded.

And his "Dallas" friends can hardly imagine life without Larry. Ken Kercheval recalled visiting him at the Inn at Turtle Creek, where Larry now stays during the "Dallas" shootings. He was greeted by Larry, who sat on the balcony and blasted away on a tuba. Linda Gray remembered that when her twenty-one-year marriage fell apart in 1983, the first to come to her doorstep were Larry and Maj. Larry brought flowers, champagne . . . and a bubble-making machine. The house filled with bright, shining bubbles, and the woman who plays Sue Ellen Ewing cried with joy. Courtesy of Larry, tragedy had become celebration.

Vita celebratio est. The flag was made by his friend and neighbor David Wayne, who believed that it captured Larry's personality. Few would deny it. The flag is only one of 200 Larry has collected; another appropriate one reads, "The Mad Monk of Malibu," which is also Larry's CB handle.

Larry began collecting flags because they helped him gauge the prevailing winds when the time came to sail his eighteen-foot Hobie Cat. The sailboat didn't last, but the flags did. Malibu Mission includes nine flagpoles, two of them higher than the rest and hoisting the two permanently flying flags: the fifty stars and stripes, and the Lone Star flag of Texas.

Today, when a visitor travels to Malibu to see the Hagmans, he'll often find the flag of his state or country greeting him. Larry particularly enjoys the colorful flags from developing countries, and decorates his flagpoles as he does himself: according to random impulse.

As his legacy, Larry has contemplated opening "The Hagman Museum of Eclectic Idiosyncrasies." In addition to the flags and the gorilla costumes, the museum would also include Larry's 500 hats. As with the flags, there's a practical origin behind Larry's fetish. Being a fair-skinned boy in the Weatherford days, he usually wore a cap to protect himself from getting burned. He began collecting in the late fifties, when he read somewhere that the sun could do everlasting damage to your skin. Since that time, Larry's collection has grown, primarily due to gifts ranging from a British bobby's hat (from Mary) to the hats Ronald Reagan handed over when it came time for the politician to move from California to the White House in 1980. Other favorites include the derby Burgess Meredith brought back from England, a Mao cap, gourd hats and palm-frond hats from the Philippines.

"Hats have different social values," Larry said. "A bowler in London says you're a distinguished person, but in New York it means you're a snob. You can fit into different societies just by changing hats. It makes cruising easier."

But it's hard to imagine what society Larry intends to fit into when he cruises the streets of Dallas while wearing a fireman's hat, complete with flashing light and blaring siren.

"Every time I go to a foreign country, I bring Larry back hats for his collection," said Peter Fonda. "Also medals. This guy is really into medals. I got him a rare one that only guys like Douglas MacArthur ever wore— the American Foreign Service Medal, given out by the government of the Philippines to military commanders. He wears it on his jackets, coats, tuxedos, bathing suits— both on formal occasions and at beach parades."

There might not be enough room in The Hagman Museum of Eclectic Idiosyncrasies to include the family's land cruiser, but the vehicle is every bit as offbeat as Larry's gorilla costumes. The cruiser is actually a converted bread van with a plastic dome, decorated with Moroccan trappings complete with incense, and usually featuring music like belly-dance tunes on the stereo.

Larry and Maj like to travel the country in their van in search of American hot springs. Maj acquired a book once that listed every natural hot spring in the country, and the Hagmans intend to visit them all when they get a chance.

In the meantime, they've got their own family grotto, and in Larry's words: "The family that bathes together, stays together." Maj has convinced others of this as well: for a minimum of $12,000, clients like Burgess Meredith and TV producer Robert Radnitz have purchased customized versions of the Malibu Mission spa.

While it seems unlikely that Maj Hagman will ever have to be the couple's primary breadwinner, the days of "Dallas" may be numbered. In January of 1986, Bud Grant, CBS's President of Entertainment, informed TV critics that in his view, the serial drama was all but dead. CBS would no longer be signing up new serials, said Grant. He did not make mention of the fate of "Dallas," and the show's producers remarked later that they would choose not to view the remarks as a slap in the face. In fact, CBS again pulled out the stops with the 1986 cliffhanger featuring the return of Patrick Duffy.

But it may be emblematic of the times that in Houston, a mild controversy developed when CBS insisted on showing the 1986 cliff-hanger at its regularly scheduled time rather than televising the Houston Rockets–Los Angeles Lakers pro basketball playoff game. The network contended that more people were interested in "Dallas" than basketball, but the ensuing furor indicated otherwise. Or at least, it indicated that viewers could put off a "Dallas" cliff-hanger for a couple of hours. Time was when that was unthinkable.

The entire "Dallas" cast, including Larry, has signed new contracts that carry the show through the 1987 season. A number of television critics predict that at that time, "Dallas" will go the way of "Hill Street Blues," which has been slotted for dissolution after that ensemble cast's contracts expire the same year. A number of "Dallas" stars have denied this possibility, suggesting that as long as viewers keep the show in Nielsen's top ten, "Dallas" will respond with new episodes.

But as far back as 1980, when Larry was riding a tide of international fame, the "Dallas" star was bracing himself for the end. Remembering how far he fell after the cancellation of "I Dream of Jeannie," Larry remarked, "I know this, too, will end."

Larry Hagman could retire today a wealthy man, of course. But acting continues to be his passion, and as long as he's good at it and in good health, he sees no reason to discontinue his profession. Already, he has accumulated enough directing experience in episodes of "I Dream of Jeannie," "Dallas" and "Knots Landing" to involve himself in TV projects from all facets. The idea of producing, directing and starring in a few CBS Movies of the Week appeals to him greatly.

"Well," mused Larry on the subject of directing shows, "it's one less actor to argue with—one less big, crazy actor."

Chances are that we'll not see Larry Hagman on the big screen again. It is an unusual but reliable phenomenon that major television stars do not enjoy success in the cinema. This is partly because of television typecasting, partly due to a loss in credibility because of having worked in television for so long, and partly because of the new competition: the De Niros, the Streeps, the Hoffmans and the Redfords.

"Movies, for me, don't make that much money," said Larry. "I make several millions of dollars a year in television. Nobody has ever asked me to make a movie for $10 million. Plus the competition . . . I have to do what I do best or most lucratively. You reach a lot more people with television than with movies."

Of course, Larry could always find other ways of making money. "I've got some forty old scripts annotated with bullshit from a bunch of TV creeps at the network," he told a reporter. "I'm going to sell one for fifty or a hundred bucks, set the value for tax purposes. Then I'm going to donate the whole lot to a library and take a whopping tax credit."

Spoken like a true Ewing. But Larry Hagman is just as capable of portraying himself as a regular guy who earns what he gets. "I don't gamble, I am not a womanizer, I have two great kids and have been married to the same woman for twenty-six years," he assured one interviewer in 1980. "I don't spend much on clothes, because my wife makes most of them, as well as her own. And I still spend everything before I get it."

Had J.R. Ewing never been created and delighted our imaginations, history might well have described Larry Hagman as he has described himself: a hard worker and family man. It might have made little difference to anyone that the son of Peter Pan would emerge from the inkblot city of Weatherford, Texas, and become the Mad Monk of Malibu, playing his flute on the beach with dozens of locals trailing behind him, singing gleefully along.

But we can be grateful to nasty ol' J.R. for bringing

Larry Hagman to our undivided attention, just as we can adore Hagman for his remarkable creation. Somehow they have both come to us at the right time, when we desperately need both myth and flesh, both lovable villains and bizarre heroes. They remind us that the complexities of life don't have to be agonizing. They can be *fun*.

Don't worry. Be happy. Feel good. Vita celebratio est. The pleasure's all his, darlin'.

Index

INDEX

INDEX